RUN
FOR YOUR LIFE

RUN FOR YOUR LIFE

Dr. Art Mollen

A Dolphin Book
DOUBLEDAY & COMPANY, INC.
GARDEN CITY, NEW YORK
1978

ISBN: 0-385-13257-3

Library of Congress Catalog Card Number: 77-78517

Copyright © 1978 by Arthur J. Mollen and Steven Englund
All Rights Reserved
Printed in the United States of America

First Edition

This book has been dedicated to two people, one living and one deceased.

The one living would be my most loving wife who has been the greatest inspiration to me in writing this book. She has provided me with the motivation, enthusiasm, encouragement, and warmth to convey a message to everyone.

The one deceased is my father, Samuel Jean Mollen, deceased November 10, 1972 of coronary artery disease, who has provided me with the ability to motivate and proselytize people toward good health. His generosity and kindness shall be remembered always.

ACKNOWLEDGMENTS

It is with great pleasure and gratitude that I acknowledge the contributions of Steven Englund.

I would also like to thank Patrick Filley, my editor at Dolphin Books.

CONTENTS

Chapter One	Why Running?	1
Chapter Two	Getting Started	17
Chapter Three	Priming the Pump	29
Chapter Four	Revitalizing You	43
Chapter Five	Psychological Benefits	53
Chapter Six	Practical Running	69
Chapter Seven	Excuses and Their Overcoming	87
Chapter Eight	Running Diets	107
Chapter Nine	A Running Seminar with Dr. Mollen	129
Chapter Ten	Staying With It	143
Appendix	Dr. Mollen's Guidelines to Easy Jogging	149
	Dr. Mollen's Survey of The American Medical Jogger's Association	152

RUN
FOR YOUR LIFE

Chapter One

WHY RUNNING?

If you were to come into my clinic in Phoenix, Arizona, I would put you through the same battery of tests to which I submitted a forty-seven-year-old insurance salesman who recently came to see me. Bert weighed 200 pounds, his blood pressure was 180/110 and his pulse was 86, his cholesterol count was 325, and his triglycerides, 400. In addition to these tests, I gave him an executive health profile (blood work), a chest X ray, electrocardiogram, and a stress electrocardiogram by treadmill. The results of these tests sobered both of us.

I explained to Bert that I was going to write him an exercise prescription, which he could fill only at the corner of Campbell and 16th streets in downtown Phoenix, at 6:00 A.M., Mondays, Wednesdays, and Fridays. There, I, in my pharmacist's guise, count out the number of miles to be walked or run, the time it should take, and the frequency of the exercise. (For some patients running is not the best exercise, so I recommend bicycling—stationary or outdoors—or swimming.) This pharmacy is called the Preventive Medicine and Physical Fitness Institute. Some two dozen people congregate there to take their daily dose and encourage each other. The camaraderie of the group helped to increase Bert's enthusiasm for, and interest in, the exercises. It has been my experience that the program will not "take" if it is seen as an unpleasant chore. Thus I try to expose my patients to its fun aspects.

Initially, I put Bert on an interval jogging program—slow running until a feeling of discomfort occurs, walking until the pulse slows down and normal breathing returns, slow jogging, etc. After twelve weeks he weighed 160 pounds, registered blood pressure of 130/80 and pulse of 64, and exhibited a cholesterol count of 200 and a triglyceride count of 125.

In other words, instead of treating high blood pressure with massive doses of chemicals, I am attempting to lower their vital signs with massive doses of what I call LSD—Long Slow Distance—running. When a patient first comes to my office I attempt to motivate them, explain to them the potential benefits of exercise, and remind them of the damages they can inflict on their body by being careless with it. Motivation, however, is the key. Without that inner impulse, the program I prescribe will be meaningless.

You're in my office now, simply because you have picked up this book. You've sought me out because you want to improve your physical and mental state, a way to feel well. That is what I am here for, but I must be frank with you. There are no magical cures, no pharmaceutical potions I can give you. I can show you how to trim your body and improve the functioning of your vital organs. I can make you aware of the benefits that can accrue to you from proper exercise and diet: tangible improvements—weight, appearance, fitness—at first; intangible changes—in the *quality* of your life—later. But beyond this, a few tests, and some prescriptive advice, there is really nothing *I can do to you or for you.* If anything happens, it will be because *you will do it to and for yourself.*

Once that is clear, I must tell you that we are going to embark on a permanent journey—not a trek of one week, or one month, or one year. The charts of your way to lower blood pressure, weight loss, etc., will to some extent prove to be the guidelines for living the rest of your life. *Are you willing to be fit?* Postponing fitness may not kill you on the spot, but it will likely take away from you the only chance you have for living a maximum life.

There are as many different impulses to begin serious running as there are people who begin serious running. I tend, in my practice, to meet forty-eight-year-old salesmen, like Vilas, who weigh well over 200 pounds, and have tried and failed to stick to every diet (from Atkins' to Weight Watchers) hypoed by the media; or housewives like Geraldine, whose last physician told her, "You're just a typical, obese, middle-aged, middle-class housewife. There is nothing I can do for you. You're not sick. Here's a diet. Stick to it. I'll renew your prescription for Librium. Now don't keep bothering me." Both suffered from their physical and mental ailments, but no one had ever offered them positive steps toward cure. All they had ever heard were negatives, "Stop eating so much!" or "Stop worrying!"

Many of these patients have grown a hard shell of skepticism, which may also be true of many readers of this book. Most of you will have a "Show me" attitude. But that is a far cry from the dejected and hostile Geraldine who plumped herself down in my office and told me in no uncertain terms, "I'm a very critical person. I've heard a lot of superlative things about you and your program, but frankly I find them pretty hard to believe. But I'm here because I have no place else to go. So let's see what can be done for me."

Both Vilas and Geraldine (and many, many others) have become convinced that they are "different"; that they are the truly "hopeless" case. They never are, of course; no one is. And as soon as they begin to run (or, in Vilas' case, walk), they find that pounds actually do disappear and, to their amazement, stay away. Their enthusiasm and good cheer increases in inverse proportion to the fall in their blood pressure, pulse, and cholesterol levels.

I also see young people like Bill, twenty-nine, who have concentrated on business (Bill is a very successful electronics salesman) to the point where they have slacked off caring for their bodies and appearance. Bill had become, in his words, "fat and flabby," and concerned because "girls no longer pay much attention to me."

For the most part, however, I will probably not see the readers of this book in my Phoenix clinic. I would probably meet you in the course of my social life: people who are vaguely dissatisfied, paunchy, lethargic, somewhat insecure about their appearance, or anxious about their future. You have heard about running from your friends or seen the cover of *People* featuring Lee and Farrah-Fawcett Majors running together, and you are curious about whether it will benefit you. You may be like my friend Larry, who played basketball and squash regularly, but who could never rid himself of his "gut," mostly because of the large amounts of ice cream and popcorn he ingested nightly while watching television and reading mysteries. Following his roommate's advice he began running—one mile became two, became three. Or you may be like Steve, another friend, who had shucked about forty pounds of "baby fat" but still remained flabby and undefined. He had been running a gentlemanly half-mile for about a year. I met him—upped his regimen to five, six, then nine or ten miles a day. Both men now walk around with flat stomachs, lean faces, and a great deal of pride in their appearance.

Or you may be someone like me. When I first started running (in 1969) I had just graduated from medical school. I had always been somewhat of an athlete in school: a gymnast in college, weight lifting and basketball in medical school. One day some physician friends and I decided to go out and run around the local high school track, once. I shall always carry a vivid memory of that day. I barely made it around, gasping and panting the entire 440 yards. A few of my friends could not even complete the circuit.

Once we recovered our breath (and our dignity), we began to talk about the lack of emphasis in our medical training on such crucial health items as nutrition, exercise, diet, or the whole general theory of preventive medicine. We were disgruntled and embarrassed. As physicians, we felt we should be physically fit in order to relate to our patients more adequately.

I immediately embarked on a jogging program, impelled by a recent weight gain as well as by the revelations on the high school track. For two years I ran several times a week, from one to three miles, depending on my schedule. Although this program was not that extensive, its continuity and the drastic alteration it worked on my eating habits combined to lower my weight by thirty pounds and my cholesterol level by half.

It took me two years to become fully convinced that running was the most beneficial exercise I could do—and that I needed to do it every day. Once "addicted," I ran three miles a day, every day, never missing. I upped the distance a few years later when, having read an article on the Boston Marathon, I realized the incentive it could have on my patients if their physician ran 26 miles, 385 yards without stopping. I now run three marathons a year. And though I am always interested in reducing my time from one marathon to the next, the prime motivation remains the sense of joy while running and the feel of accomplishment when I have crossed the finish line. It is a far cry from that first quarter mile.

Running has thus become an important part of my life, but it has not become my life. The case of Jerry illustrates that running, in and of itself, does not change your life—but does provide you with a strong foundation for the self-esteem necessary to get on with the restructuring.

Twenty-five years old, Jerry was the unhappy and rebellious son of a highly successful Wisconsin physician. The young man was, by his own admission, an alcoholic when he first came to see me. As he stood in front of me, I saw a tall, lethargic, slightly overweight, somewhat apathetic person. Coming to see me represented his own "acceptance of the fact that I'm an alcoholic and I want to get over it."

As we talked, it became clear to me that Jerry's problems extended beyond liquor. Indeed, alcohol was simply the final unhappy consequence of previous, deeper problems. An unhappy relationship with his father, whom Jerry greatly resented for what he felt to be the man's emotional inaccessibility and undemonstrativeness, had corroded the son's own self-image. Life was "meaningless" and "valueless" for Jerry. He had almost no motivation, and hadn't had for two years—a fact that precipitated the decline of his marriage and physical body as

Why Running?

well as his disposition. Jerry had reduced himself to the status of addict. He was a depressing sight.

I am a general practice physician, not a psychiatrist. There was no way that I could treat this young man's deep-rooted unhappiness with his father. All I could think to do was offer Jerry a *stress release*—running—which might alleviate some of his need to drink, since he rightly regarded his dependence on alcohol as his most pressing problem. This was only a hunch, a gamble on my part. There is no automatic answer to an intractable problem like alcoholism, but I thought there was a slim chance to substitute one addiction for another. Jerry had told me that he had run in college and that the experience had meant a lot to him. "It was one of the few successes I ever achieved that had nothing to do with my father," he told me. "Running really meant a lot to me." He had tried to run upon occasion since college, but with no structured program or support group, his efforts bogged down and he gave up.

My hope was that Jerry's success with a running program—*our* program—would perhaps restore some of his self-control and self-respect and thereby reduce his dependency on liquor. We started him out running a mile a day. That was three months ago. He now runs fifteen miles a day (and they're six-minute miles, I might add). He hasn't touched a drop of alcohol since he commenced the program.

Jerry is not a perfect example of the best sort of well-being runner, and I didn't include his case here for that reason. As will become clear later on in this book, I don't think compulsiveness has a place in well-being running any more than it does in any other activity of life. And Jerry's running—*always* against the clock—shows signs of compulsiveness. However, this is a small price to pay, it seems to me, for the good that has been done. In Jerry's case we were lucky enough to effect a transformation from a strong negative addiction to a strong positive one. If the compulsiveness factor stays constant for a while, that's acceptable.

Nor has Jerry lost very much weight. He still hates his father, and he still, so far as I can see, has a lot of his old problems. But to hear the boy talk, you'd think he had experienced rebirth. And for him the heart of the matter is his switch from scotch to Gatorade.

In sum, I don't think running is the answer to all of Jerry's problems; but it is clearly a damn sight better than the 80 per-cent-proof solution he'd been downing. Now, anyway, he's in a position of some strength from which, when he chooses, he can slowly confront the deeper-rooted problems of his life from which he had been previously hiding. In sum, he has begun to substitute a positive compulsion for a negative addiction.

The people for whom daily jogging in a structured program has accomplished so many wonderful things are people just like yourselves—with all your problems, self-doubts, aches, pains, hopes, and fears. They have the same kinds of jobs, live the same kinds of lives. They are no more endowed with resources of willpower and self-discipline than you are; they have no intention of trying out for the 1980 Olympic Games. They simply wanted to feel better, and they have found an activity, and a forum in which to practice it, which—though it only requires an hour or less a day—has improved their health and appearance and restored their sense of confidence, self-control, and general well-being.

You too want to feel better, or else why would your

Why Running?

feet have carried you past the mystery and best-seller racks and toward the sports and fitness section of the bookstore? Ensconced now in your easy chair, you have entered a "branch office" of my Phoenix clinic. You are still able and unimpaired, but you are worried. If I am to be of help to you, you must transfer that worry into commitment. More, you are still wholeheartedly committed to your schedule of work, achievement, success, self-indulgence, and abuse. I need some of that commitment also. The once-a-week tennis match isn't what I mean, nor the weekend round of golf, even eighteen holes on both Saturday and Sunday. I need more from you than that, but I can promise, in return, a pleasant, not terribly difficult experience.

What I am going to prescribe for you presently will make a difference; or, rather, it will give *you* the chance to make a difference for yourself. I cannot oblige you to follow through on my prescription any more than an architect can oblige you to adhere to his blueprints, but I can promise that *if you do*, there is no question it will make for a quick and radical change in your life. The change will be not merely physical but attitudinal—your outlook on your work, your enjoyment of leisure, your relationships with people, loved ones, and friends—will all be affected. Your life will have more life; its *quality* will be improved.

What do we mean by *quality* of life? Well, many things, but initially it might boil down to one word: control. Control is the one thing we haven't been able to fabricate or nourish or even salvage and maintain in our society. The autonomy and individualism of our founding fathers are things of the past. We can fly to the moon, land a module on Mars, and we have automatic toothbrushes, but we are daily losing the sense of centered will, of self-control, of self-reliance which any human life requires to fulfill itself.

We are the self-made prisoners of the innumerable gadgets, forces, stimuli, institutions, conventions, expectations, demands, obligations, habits, needs, and instincts that constitute (without filling) a person's life. We imagine ourselves at the center of this complicated cockpit of drives and choices steering our own path. In actual fact, we are being driven.

This feeling of being out of control is irritating and depressing. It saps our self-assurance while it leaves us restless and baffled. When we try to deal with it by arbitrarily asserting authority in some area—e.g., stopping smoking, not shouting at the kids, standing up to the boss, going on a diet, reading a book a week, etc.—the effort begins with a trumpet fanfare but peters out after a week, leaving us with a redoubled sense of our own impotency before the blind forces that govern our lives.

You can avoid the extremes of unhappy resignation on the one hand, or flight and irresponsibility on the other. A middle way, a better way is possible; a self-willed path that can lead you through the obstacles and responsibilities of life without giving way or giving up.

The way is running—not occasional running, or short-term running in pursuit of ulterior goals, not competitive running, or running against the clock, but running as a daily activity of the whole self, running where the lessons and consciousness of the run slowly pervade the whole of your life. It is my belief that those who commence a program of steadily lengthening jogs will soon find themselves being weaned away from the sharpest pangs of aimlessness, boredom, and frustration—and disabusing

Why Running?

themselves of the material and monetary attempts to relieve those conditions, and replacing them with a more positive state of mind. I call this the philosophy of running LSD—Long Slow Distance. The theory was developed by a German physiologist, Ernst Van Aaken, who tells us that eventually we must learn to run as children, children at play; that is, to walk, jog, and run in serious fun.

Running is better for you than tennis, golf, racketball, or volleyball because it is continuous exercise; it is more convenient and accessible than swimming—after all, how many of us have olympic-sized pools in our back yards? Running is much less expensive than skiing; it is more fun than sit-ups, and less dangerous than football or rugby. For the price of a quantum of willpower, a dole of time, and twenty to thirty dollars, you will be equipped to set foot on that middle path I mentioned above.

There are many signposts on that road, and I shall detail them in later chapters. Suffice it for now to mention the sense of accomplishment ("I *can* do it"), the changed dimensions of your body ("My God, have you lost weight!" or "None of my pants fit me anymore!"), your increasing concern with what you put into your body ("Norma, throw out the Doritos and the Ding-Dongs"), and, most important, the new state of consciousness you achieve about yourself as ever-increasing distances separate you, temporally and spiritually, from the patterns of your everyday life.

In a nutshell, running provides you with mental and physical endurance. Endurance is more important than strength. It's that fillip we need at 4:00 in the afternoon of a slow day when we want to go home but duty tells us to sell five more policies, or see four more patients, or call three more customers. Mostly we need endurance for the sake of our heart so that it pumps only 45-55 times a minute to accomplish the same tasks that other people's hearts need 80-90 beats to do.

If two people walk up a steep hill, the man with endurance will register a pulse increase of approximately 40 beats per minute. The person without endurance will find his heart jumping 80 or 90 beats above normal (and his normal is already twice that of the fit person). The heart of an out-of-condition person is working far less efficiently than the heart of a runner and is using too much energy to accomplish only moderately difficult tasks.

Endurance is one thing running gives you. Immunization against heart disease is another. If you run regularly, your chances of dropping by the wayside as many of your friends and colleagues might do are greatly diminished. Regular jogging also promises considerable protection from a whole roster of the so-called diseases of civilization: ulcers, hypertension, insomnia, lung problems, kidney ailments, etc.

Your symptoms and your "tests" indicate that you *need* endurance; you *need* immunization. You are sitting on a physiological time bomb. That explosion, when it comes, could be mental and attitudinal, by the way, as well as physical. A combination of stress, pressure, indulgence, and sedentary habits can overwhelm your consciousness as surely as they sap your heart and blood vessels. Some of your friends may have had the explosion already: fits of depression, periods of ennui, anxiety attacks, nervous breakdowns, excessive drug use, etc.

So look around at your possessions and accomplishments and ask yourself what they count for next to your health and life. How much of your time and energy

Why Running?

goes into attaining goals and acquiring objects whose worth pales into insignificance next to the full use of a sound body and a clear mind? I'll wager it was a lot more time and energy than you put into caring for and appreciating the body that gives you movement, sensation, speech, life. Ask yourself: Is this fair to me? Is it safe? Is it likely to provide me with much long-term satisfaction?

Dedicated running, then, offers you immunization against cardiovascular problems and a preventative against psychological desuetude. As important as these benefits are, nevertheless they are still the lesser half of what LSD offers. The more positive side is improved quality of life, a concept I have already touched on and to which I shall return again and again. For now, however, the point is to start you running; to encourage you to begin thinking about the creation of habits, patterns, even of addiction to my brand of LSD.

Habits, in case you haven't discovered, are neither easy to break nor to start. The habits of diet and exercise I will be discussing shortly are not unduly arduous nor demanding in themselves. They do not require herculean efforts of willpower. (Nor, for that matter, will the strength of Goliath be required to break your old sedentary or gluttonous habits.) They do require some effort. Effort, it must be stressed, which will be repaid in full by the joy and satisfaction that will suffuse you as running begins to transform you into a new person. I've watched it happen time and again in people just like you.

So be of stout heart and good cheer because you have the choice. It isn't that often in life anymore that we are aware of choice; and yet the innumerable choices of everyday life are the clay from which we mold the material of our lives. The choices, decisions, and options come at us in such number and are resolved with so little ado, that we forget they are indeed choices. It is absolutely essential, therefore, to remind ourselves every so often: *We have a say in who and what we are.*

The choice is between full life or half life. I want to stress the "full" in front of life. I challenge you with more than the threat of despondency, disablement, or death. I challenge you with the possibility of a more complete life.

The pep talk is over. From here on, I am presuming a minimum of enthusiasm and co-operation from you. I can continue to write in this vein, and you can continue to sit in your recliner and read, but words alone are insufficient to emphasize the beneficial effect of running. As you leaf through this book even now, my single overriding desire is to have you jump out of your chair and take a short jog. Don't think about it, or plan on doing it sometime, or even imagine what a wonderful world it would be "if only I jogged regularly." *I just want you to do it.* Now. Don't go on to the next sentence. Put down the book. Go run, jog, slog, or walk a mile or whatever distance you can do without discomfort, and then come back and pick up where you left off. *But do it.* Don't put it off. Don't lay long-range or medium-range plans . . . at least not yet. They're too easy to default on in the beginning. Get some experience under your belt right off the bat; prove to yourself that you have the willpower and self-control to run a distance. You'll feel much better for the effort, simply having shown yourself you're in control—that you can do it. It will lay a more important foundation for the rest of your life than hours of leafing through books on self-help and health. You're off . . .

Chapter Two

GETTING STARTED

Now you're back. Doesn't the sweat feel good? Let it drip down your brow; don't wipe it away too quickly. That's good sweat. You probably didn't run too far, did you? Don't worry, very few do until they get conditioned. What you don't have now—endurance—is precisely what running will give you, along with many other rewards. For the moment, cool off, take a shower, and then return to talk with me. Before you embark on your second, third, and ongoing days of running there are a few things you should know about the art of joggery, or, as my patients and friends humorously put it, "the joggery of art."

RUNNERS, GET READY . . .

The first thing to do is to make yourself aware that running, like any other regular pattern or habit, will require proper attention to appropriate equipment. I do not mean simply shorts or sweat suits and sneakers. Sneakers are fine for the first few runs, but they are not designed to protect and cushion the foot from the stress of the pounding it takes from a regular running program. I will go into the question of proper attire and the selection of shoes in Chapter Six.

The second thing to do is set up a running course so you know exactly where you're going to run and how far. I would suggest that you map out a fairly level one-mile distance that will start and end at your house. You may want to make it only a half-mile course in the beginning; or you may wish to run the mile "out" and walk the mile "in."

You should pick the least-traveled roads. If it is necessary for you to run on or near main thoroughfares, slow down and yield for crossing traffic. If you run at dawn or dusk, wear white so that you are visible to drivers. Runners and bicyclers face the same problem on our city streets—drivers are not looking for them.

Let Frank Shorter and Lasse Viren tackle the toughest hills and ruggedest terrain in your area. For now, your concern should be with runable distances and manageable topography. On the other hand, try to select a course that offers some interesting scenery (or at least varying scenery) as this helps conquer that omnipresent tempter, boredom.

Hard-packed dirt (such as on most high school or college running tracks or municipal park bridle paths) is the best surface. It is smooth and the dirt allows a certain "slide" effect which cuts down on blisters and friction. Pavement and asphalt is equally smooth but, during the summer especially, can be very hot and wearing on the soles of the feet. Grass is cooler and springier than dirt or asphalt, but it hides uneven terrain, potholes, etc., which can cause strains and sprains.

Whatever the surface, do not elongate the course beyond a mile. In other words, do not try to bite off more than you can chew. On the contrary, from a psychological point of view it will be better if the effort is a fairly easy

Getting Started

one at first. One or two miles a day, taken at *any* pace, is 100 per cent better than nothing. Remember, in the beginning it does not matter how you cover the distance. *What is of lasting importance is that you cover the ground you've laid out.*

AT SUNUP OR SUNDOWN?

Unless you live in a desert climate—as I do in Phoenix—where early morning running is a practical necessity, the best time for you to run is *anytime*. Find the time of day that best suits your metabolism and life-style. However, through long experience with beginning runners, such as you, I have learned that jogging in the morning is the best way to insure that you get your daily running in. The beginner is especially prone to a search for excuses, and the course of a normal working day will provide the diligent seeker with all manner of pretexts to avoid running—"I'm too tired," "My mind's not on it," "We're already late for dinner with Fred and Sally." The events and stimuli of a long day can be exhausting and distracting. Don't risk not running. *Do it early.*

There is also something about the beauty of an early morning run that cannot be communicated to someone who has not experienced it. The play of the dew, the sun, and the cold on your freshly awakened senses is wonderfully invigorating. Moreover, morning running (before breakfast, naturally) gives the novice a sense of discipline and accomplishment. He or she knows that even before opening the newspaper or driving to the office, something important has been completed. That feeling lasts and sustains one throughout the course of an otherwise tiring, irritating day. In any event, for what statistical samples are worth, studies have shown that 75 per cent of beginning runners who run in the morning stick with their jogging program beyond the initial stage. Only 50 per cent of afternoon runners stay with it, and half that percentage (25 per cent) of night joggers hang on.

Nevertheless, some people really do prefer late-in-the-day jogging. They are night owls in their metabolism, and it would be the height of discomfort for them to jump out of bed and into their Adidas. Or they may well look forward to a late-afternoon run as an excellent way to unwind from the stress and fatigue of a long day of work. They usually discover that afterward they are invigorated and energized, ready to do more in the course of an evening than watch television. (The joys of running toward a setting sun are not to be dismissed, either.)

RUNNERS, TO YOUR MARKS . . .

As you are pulling on your sweat socks and shoes the image flashes into your mind of the people down at the office who have just taken up running. They have been complaining (loudly) of aching muscles, cramped tendons, pains in the knees and lower back, etc. Or your memory may be jogged by some other books or articles on the subject in which some of the sport's greatest advocates, practitioners, and writers proclaim the agony of jogging as if it were some sort of badge of courage. They make it sound as if pain is innate to running.

Well, it's not. (So stop peeling off your running gear.)

The cause of the large majority of aches and pains is tight muscles. *All* muscles lose their flexibility and elastic-

Getting Started 23

ity when they are inactive (i.e., when we are sedentary). If, suddenly, you leap up and run one or two miles, with no preparation of the muscles, they will naturally feel the strain . . . and will let you know they feel it. You are even risking tearing or rupturing a muscle or ligament.

Muscles, thus, need to be conditioned for a few minutes before you start your run. "Stretchies," as I call them, take almost no time, but they protect you from a lot of aches and a lot of risks. *Do not neglect them; do them every time you run.*

Begin by bending at the waist and allowing your trunk to hang roughly parallel with the ground. Do this until you feel a bit of tension in your lower back and legs. That means the muscles are stretching. Above all, don't bounce up and down, as you may be tempted to do because you see athletes doing it. Bouncing could strain or pull a muscle. Simply hang over and count slowly to 20.

Then stand on your tiptoes and reach your arms into the air as high as you can for another 20-count.

Next, stand up straight and turn your torso, twisting at the waist in both directions several times.

Then stretch your hands out in front of you pressing against a wall with your heels and feet flat on the ground. Do 10 push-ups into the wall, thus stretching the tendons in the back of your legs (calves and heels).

Next, standing balanced on your toes on the edge of a step (as if you were going to do a back somersault dive), move up and down on your toes with the arches and heels of your feet hanging in space. That, too, will stretch the all-important heel tendons.

Now you need a rest, so sit down on the floor. Place your right leg out in front of you with the sole of your left foot touching the inside of your right upper leg. Then reach all the way forward and grab your right foot with your hands and hold on for a 20-count. Repeat the procedure with the right foot placed inside the outstretched left leg.

Finally, with the soles of your feet together in front of you, push gently down on both knees and hold this position for 20 seconds. Staying in the same position, lower your head as far toward your feet as you can for 10 seconds.

Now you're finished, and it didn't take more than 4 or 5 minutes, but the time was well spent because it has dramatically reduced the likelihood of your incurring pain and injury during your run. By the way, you needn't do all these stretch exercises each time you run, but make sure you do most of them.

GET SET . . .

As you open the front door and step outside, you will probably begin to wonder about pace. Do not worry about speed—at least not until you have been running regularly for several months. The philosophy of LSD running puts no emphasis whatever on how long it takes you to cover the distance you've laid out for yourself. On the contrary, concern for improvement in running time is one of the best ways I know to put a stitch in the side of your running program before you've actually gotten it going. The physical and mental goals you are looking for in daily jogging do not mesh well with any kind of compulsiveness, least of all one that focuses on the running itself.

In this same vein, don't worry or concentrate overly on your form and its fine points. Don't constantly ask your-

Getting Started

self, "Am I doing something wrong? Should my elbows rise this high? Should my fists be open or clenched? How many steps should I take per minute? How high should I raise my knees?" etc. The answers to these and a thousand related questions don't matter at this point. Just run and stop thinking.

Finally, get used to the idea that the first few minutes of your daily run will *always* prove somewhat uncomfortable. Bear up, it will subside. Every runner, from Roger Bannister to Frank Shorter, experiences the same unpleasantness you do as the body and metabolism rapidly move from static equilibrium to high-level oxygen consumption. The metamorphosis is never easy, but you get accustomed to running through it.

GO! . . .

As you run, slip into an easy stride. Don't run too fast. (Follow the motto of the San Francisco Dolphin South End runners: "Start slow and then taper off.") A good rule of thumb about speed: Don't run faster than you can comfortably hold a conversation with a fellow runner (or with an imaginary fellow runner). To run too fast at this stage is to court certain breathlessness because your cardiopulmonary (heart/lung) system has not yet been conditioned to sudden, greatly increased demands of oxygen. Getting winded is very uncomfortable and proves to be a major reason why beginners quickly become discouraged and want to quit after the first quarter mile.

As you run, concentrate on your chief goal: *covering the distance you have set for yourself* (usually one mile in the beginning). The time it takes doesn't matter, though as the weeks fly by, you'll be pleased to note your speed increases. Don't calculate your form to impress anyone; don't see yourself as Jesse Owens streaking down the track. In the early stage of developing an addiction to running, you almost have to look bad to look (and feel) good. Keep your arms loose and relaxed at your sides. It doesn't matter if they flail out a bit. Bend them if you like, but not in tense acute angles with clenched fists pumping to shoulder level.

Let your foot strike the ground heel-toe, not vice versa. This last point is important. Many beginners will want to copy the sprinters they have watched on TV or at track meets by running on the balls of their feet, knees raised high. Admittedly, this running posture is impressive—a kind of lightning prance—but it's useless for our purposes. Biomechanically the heel-toe step is best for long-term jogging, because the leg muscles do not contract as much as in the ball-of-the-foot landing and because there is a natural "rocking" motion in heel-toe, which provides more rhythm and less strain.

You will tend to lapse into ball- or flat-footed landings since most of your experience with running has been of the sprinting variety common to the sandlots and playing fields of your youth. But keep the heel-toe in mind as the technique favored by almost three fourths of the world's professional runners.

THE FINISH LINE

In the flush of excitement which has ensued from your second day's efforts, do not race up to your door and flop into your favorite chair with an ice-cold beverage in

Getting Started

hand. It is good practice to build a winding-down segment into your run. Either slow your pace for the last 300 yards, or if you like to sprint the last lap to show yourself how much you have left, walk around until your breathing has returned to normal. Biologically, the slackened pace is necessary to give the cardiovascular system time to redistribute the blood supply from the legs, where most of it has gone during the run, back to the rest of the body.

After your shower, fill in your chart. By all means, keep a chart of your progress. It is highly motivating. The goals you want to achieve through jogging should be written down, including a program of how much you intend to increase your mileage, how many pounds (and inches) you want to lose, and much less importantly, how your running times are improving. (You might also mark down any difficulties you encountered during the run.) I know many experienced long-distance runners who keep such records year in and year out and derive great satisfaction from them.

The principal points of this jogging program can be summed up in six principles—the six S's:

Supervision—Make sure, particularly if you are over thirty-five, that your doctor has tested you informally or with the EKG-stress machine so that you know you are in physical condition to jog. Let your physician know how much you plan to run, under what conditions, where, when, etc. Ideally, he will not only be sympathetic, but interested and involved. If he is not, i.e., if he won't supervise your running program in a general sort of way, find a health professional who is knowledgeable and encouraging.

Shoes—Purchase shoes made for runners, make sure the

fit is snug, keep them in good repair (especially the heels).

Stretching—Don't forget the "stretchies." Ever.

Surface—Avoid asphalt and concrete as much as possible. It's hard on the feet and ankles. Try to run on dirt, grass, or tartan track. Avoid rocky and bumpy ground; you risk sprains.

Speed—Slow and comfortable.

Slacken off—Wind down your pace before you sit down or take a shower.

Chapter Three

PRIMING THE PUMP

So far, you have been propelled along in your running program on faith or hope. At some point, however, you are going to begin to wonder what, physiologically speaking, running does for you and how it does it? Every observer, from the most casual to the most rigorous and systematic, agrees that a daily running program, by lowering the pulse rate, blood pressure readings, and cholesterol levels of the runner, increases the efficiency of the cardiovascular (heart and blood) system and, thereby, insures longer, healthier lives.

The evidence is clear—no matter the culture observed. The Tarahumara Indians of North Central Mexico, for example, have been, over the course of many generations, running distances of up to a hundred miles without stopping. A study, published in the February 1976 edition of *The Physician and Sportsmedicine*, found a significant relationship between the cardiovascular capacity and endurance of the Indians and their distance running.

In our own society, two investigators from San Diego State University, Fred Kasch and Janet Wallace, recently concluded a ten-year study of the effects of an exercise program on a group of men who began the program at the age of forty-five. For the ensuing decade the men exercised three times a week for one hour at a time. Thirteen of the men ran, two combined swimming and running, one swam. When the men were retested after ten years, it was found that their hearts were able to pump as well as they had at the age of forty-five. Their lung functioning had improved, and their resting heart rate and blood pressure remained constant.

I myself conducted a survey of 100 physicians, all of whom have run at least one marathon (26.2 mile) race. Every single one of them gave his *professional* opinion, speaking as a doctor not simply a jogger, that running makes a major difference in improving a patient's cardiovascular system. Eighty-five per cent of the physicians said that running six miles a day will provide cardiopulmonary immunization from disease.

In my own practice, blood pressure improvements are the most dramatic—and consistent—evidence of the benefits of a running program. High blood pressure is the sign of a heart that is working overtime—because of inefficiency or excess stress—to supply the body with its normal blood needs. Over a long period of time, high blood pressure puts excessive strain on the heart muscle—taxes it beyond endurance. Most of my patients suffer from hypertension; until they start running, that is. Earl, within a six-week period (during which he increased his distance from one to five miles a day), saw his blood pressure drop from 160/110 to 130/80. Martha, a fifty-six-year-old woman, lowered her blood pressure to 108/80 from 152/100; John, a retired Air Force officer, went from 158/98 to 118/80.

Your body is like a machine. It needs energy to work. The more efficiently it burns up the energy available to it, the longer it will last and the more qualitatively it will "produce." The body's energy is measured in units called

Priming the Pump

calories which come from the food we eat. The burning of these calories to produce energy requires oxygen, which is carried by the blood and pumped by the heart. As more work is done, more oxygen is required to burn the required extra calories. So you breathe harder to take in more oxygen.

The signs of hard-working lungs and hearts—shorter breaths, pounding heart, perspiration—were readily apparent to you thirty seconds into your first run. The muscles require oxygen to burn the calories needed to allow you to put one foot in front of the other. The lungs and heart work at an accelerated pace to provide that oxygen. Thus the thumping you feel in your chest and the gasping for breath. The perspiration is a sign that your body is rapidly heating up from the exertion and needs to be cooled—by the opening of the body's vents, its skin pores. (Perspiring is also a means for the body to eliminate the wastes accumulated from increased oxygen burning as well as a means of taking in more oxygen.)

As you continue running, your heart beats faster. For people who are not used to running, however, the heart very quickly begins to lag in its task of supplying the body's oxygen needs. The heart of a beginner is simply not accustomed to working hard; as a result, although its rate of beats per minute increases, its efficiency does not increase—on the contrary, it diminishes somewhat. That is, each contraction of the heart muscle of an inexperienced runner pumps out far less blood into the system (hence, less oxygen for the muscles to burn) than one contraction of the heart of a physically fit person.

The question of the heart's *efficiency* in pumping, then, is a crucial gradient in all activity. The amount of blood passing through the heart in one minute is known as "cardiac output." For our purposes it is a less important measurement than the volume of blood the heart pumps with each contraction—the "stroke volume." This is the factor that has been shown time and again to be improvable by exercise.

A person who has followed a regular program of vigorous exercise has a larger stroke volume than one who has not. The fit person can do more work with less cardiac effort and less risk of cardiac shutdown due to overwork. That person also has a larger *maximum oxygen consumption rate* than the unfit; his cardiopulmonary system (heart and lungs) can take in and process larger amounts of oxygen per minute over a larger surface of the body than the system of an unfit person can.

Runners, through constant efforts to surpass yesterday's distance and pace—by challenging themselves on a regular basis—develop larger lung capacities, larger breathing capacities, larger hemoglobin (i.e., oxygen-carrying elements in the blood) capacities, and more extensive capillarization of active muscles than non-runners. Runners also carry considerably less body fat and less cholesterol than non-runners. The LSD runner's certificate of fitness is his or her ability to work longer with vastly less energy expenditure than the average person.

Consider those benefits as you, the beginning runner, become more and more breathless during your first run until the discomfort is so great that you are obliged to stop (usually in a fit of panting). In exercise, as in longevity and good health, the key factor is efficient breathing. The breathlessness that you, as a beginning runner, feel is a sign that your cardiovascular system is not up to the sudden, large demands being made upon it. The obvious

Priming the Pump

question that occurs, especially to a runner gasping noisily after only one-half mile's exertion, is, "Why make such large, sudden demands?"

The answer is loud and clear. A sedentary life-style is a sure-fire way to end up with heart, lung, and vascular problems when you are middle-aged. Dr. George Sheehan, perhaps the best-known "running doc" in America, reports that an actuarial study of 110,000 people showed that physically active men had 50 per cent fewer heart attacks than inactive men. In England, too, according to Sheehan, a study of civil servants produced similar findings: vigorously active men had one-third the number of cases of coronary artery disease as those who were sedentary.

Dr. Alexander Leaf of the Harvard Medical School visited five human societies where extraordinary longevity had been recorded. In each instance, Dr. Leaf noted that the long lives of the people he observed and studied correlated closely to the amount of daily physical activity each person performed. Dr. Leaf himself was so humiliated at his inability to keep up with a Himalayan twice his age (the doctor was fifty-two) during a mountain hike that, upon returning to Harvard, he took up daily long-distance running.

In short, running or exercise or sports are obviously not the only times when the human system makes heavy demands on itself for rapid oxygenation. As you know from experience, any number of daily experiences—cheering at a football game, arguing with the boss or your wife or child, elation over a salary raise, sudden displays of strong emotions, etc.—will entail rapid increase of heartbeats in even the most sedentary person.

And most of us come up against frequent tasks and challenges of an immediately physical sort—mowing the lawn, making love, changing a tire, playing with the kids, etc.—which also demand sustained cardiovascular work. It would be a truly extraordinary, and most unfortunate, human life that missed out on the emotion and activity which accompany most of the key events of life.

More to the point, however, even if you could contrive to squeak through existence making minimal demands on your blood-pumping system, you'd only be insuring its long-term weakness, not strength. The heart, as we all know, is a muscle not a machine. It improves with use; it doesn't wear out or run down. Physical inactivity permits the build-up of fatty deposits in your arteries—deposits called cholesterol plaques. It is not certain exactly what causes cholesterol to build up on arterial walls and cause embolisms or occlusions or hardening of the arteries; but there is a great deal of evidence which indicates that a high level of cholesterol in the blood predisposes a person to heart trouble.

There is also a lot of evidence to connect cholesterol plaque build-up with the speed of the blood's flow throughout the heart and the vascular system. The effect of increased and sustained vascular output—i.e., from daily oxygen-burning activity—is to obstruct and diminish plaque build-up, as well as to reduce dramatically the cholesterol level in the blood. Thus, sedentary living seriously raises the risk of heart attack due to clogged arteries, especially the coronary arteries feeding the heart.

The only sure and lasting means available to people to combat the cholesterol build-up process—which varies among people according to their genetic predispositions to it, but which can be slowed down for everyone—is not chemical or medical treatment, but the disciplined training of the heart through daily oxygen-burning workouts, of which the single best known form is running.

The latest research on cholesterol has uncovered the existence of lipoproteins, bodily substances that can be divided into high- and low-density categories. The high-density lipoproteins function as removers of cholesterol from the major coronary arteries. Tests have proved that people with a very low incidence of heart disease have a significant amount of high-density lipoproteins. Documentation also exists to show that regular exercise and running increases the amount of high-density lipoproteins in one's bloodstream.

My patients have, in this area, exhibited improvement as marked as that in blood pressure rates. Decreases of 30–40 per cent are usual, but I have witnessed cuts of 50 per cent.

Physicians differ as to what constitutes "normal" levels of blood pressure and cholesterol. Many base their standards on statistics garnered from the general population. I, on the other hand, establish my standards of normalcy on a more restricted population: those people who have a zero incidence of heart disease. Thus, my normal blood pressure is 110/70 (laboratory normal is 120/80); my maximum acceptable cholesterol level is 150 mg. (laboratories accept 150–300 mg. as normal).

The cases of cardiac rehabilitation stand among the most dramatic illustrations of the positive transformations wrought by running. In case after case, people whose lives have been blighted by heart attacks, coronary artery congestion, and the like—people who could barely walk ten paces without panting for breath—have, through jogging, rebuilt their cardiopulmonary capacity from ground zero to a degree of strength and efficiency far superior to what they were before their coronary event took place. It is not unknown, nor even terribly unusual, for ex-heart victims to become successful, even established long-distance runners and marathoners.

In Santa Barbara, thirty-eight cardiac patients with blood circulation so poor many of them could barely walk one hundred feet were put on an exercise program. Six months later all the patients were jogging and "so effective was the regimen that several angina patients preparing for triple coronary bypass open-heart surgery tested normal in four to twelve weeks."

While in Arizona, William Stone conducted a similar six-month experiment with twelve cardiac rehabilitation patients as exercisers and ten as sedentaries. The exercise group, after a three-day-a-week program of exercise and jogging, tested significantly lower in resting heart rate and blood pressure; the control group showed no improvement.

The most startling illustration of the effect of serious running I have seen is the case of Tommy Rongos, fifty-five. He suffered from near-complete blockage of the coronary arteries. His physicians had strongly urged bypass surgery. Instead, Rongos entered a cardiac rehabilitation program oriented largely around running. One year later he ran the Boston Marathon.

These cases should indicate that—television commercials and magazine advertisements to the contrary notwithstanding—you are not designed for an existence of physical ease and inactivity. As physicians, anthropologists, and coaches know, human beings have an *en-*

Priming the Pump

ergy physiology underlying the structure and function of their bodily systems. Our ancestors, the inhabitants of the first 99 per cent of humankind's million-year-old history on this planet, relied heavily on the body as an efficient producer of energy to sustain them in their roles as nomads, hunters, and gatherers. Our society of leisure is a relatively new development.

The genetic and physical heritage of hundreds of thousands of years cannot be reversed in the short space of three or four generations. Our consciousness and psychology may call out for bucket seats, reclining chairs, and moving sidewalks, but our bodies are fundamentally still those of workers. Our energy physiology needs to be utilized. Our muscles and sinews and physical potential, the efficient functioning of our most critical body systems, require development or ultimately they will fall into disrepair and eventually shut down the entire organism in death.

This emphasis on your heart, lungs, and vascular system has not been unintentional. They collectively constitute the systemic kingpin of your physical body. Problems here—and there are an infinite variety of them—aren't just irritations and blemishes, they are indications of grave, very possibly mortal, infirmities. Of the top four causes of death in this country, three are closely related to the functioning of your cardiovascular system. You simply cannot afford to neglect its care and maintenance. Don't wait until after you have had a heart attack. Although running rehabilitation programs have proven very effective, the pain and expense of intensive hospital care can be avoided. Get into rehabilitating yourself now while you still have the opportunity for maximum health.

There are a number of key elements which collectively

"cause" heart disease. A list of them would look something like this:

1. *Genetic predisposition.* Is there a history of cardiac disease in your family?
2. *Personality type.* Are you what is called "Type A," i.e., a competer, a worrier, a striver, given to bouts of anxiety, stress, etc.?
3. *Life-style.* Active or sedentary?
4. *Smoking.* Do you or don't you?
5. *Alcohol.* Do you drink a lot, a little, or none at all?
6. *Overweight.* Are you?
7. *Eating habits.* Do you eat a lot of salt, carbohydrates, and cholesterol-building foods (e.g., milk, eggs, cheese, etc.)?
8. *Cholesterol count.* High or low?

You have probably noticed that seven out of eight of these elements are either directly or indirectly affected by the running program I have outlined. Except for genetic predisposition, which obviously nothing can alter, *you can do something important on every other count* . . . and you can do it, not with tranquilizers, blood-thinners, or bypass surgery, but with my program of diet and daily jogging.

Let me repeat: The main physical and physiological consequence of running is on your heart, lungs, and vascular system, and—through them—to a whole host of other bodily areas, parts, and functions (kidneys, liver, stomach, muscles, nervous system, etc.). While no hard scientific evidence yet exists to incontrovertibly prove that daily jogging immunizes you from cardiac disorder, the preponderant mass of data strongly points in that direction. Dr. Jack Scaff, Director of the Cardiac Rehabilitation Clinic in Honolulu, writes, "We are saying that once someone gets into marathon condition, the possibility of heart disease is so remote as to be negligible. We're dealing in what we think might be absolute protection."

Chapter Four

REVITALIZING YOU

The increased physiological capacities discussed in the last chapter will begin to register in your consciousness within a week or two of starting your running program. You will soon notice, for example, that your pulse rate increases much more gradually than it did when you first ran—reflecting the increased stroke volume of your heart. At rest, you will notice that your normal resting pulse rate has fallen impressively below what it used to be—reflecting the heart's greater efficiency in keeping the system supplied with blood and oxygen.

The pulse is an interesting and important measure of fitness and can serve as a convenient register of the impact running is having on your physiology. Take your own pulse right now. Place your index and middle fingers at the angle of your jaw and neck and feel the pulsations of blood circulating through the carotid artery. Count them for ten seconds and multiply the sum by six. That will give you your resting pulse rate per minute. If it is much over 76 for males or 72 for females, that is a pretty fair indication that you are out of shape.

Within a month of daily running (that is, when you have progressed to fifteen- or twenty-minute jogs daily) your pulse rate will probably have fallen off by as many as eight or ten beats a minute when you are at rest. This decline will continue as you continue to run, until your pulse reaches a base—somewhere between 40 and 60.

It is a good idea to test your pulse rate while you are running to see how high it climbs. You should wait until you are ten to fifteen minutes into your run, since, as a result of your increasing fitness, it takes the pulse rate longer to climb than it did at first. You will probably find that your pulse rate is well over a hundred. There is a standard formula for determining how high the pulse should go to condition the heart without endangering it. Take your age—say, 35—and subtract it from the number 220, leaving—in this case—a remainder of 185, which you should multiply by 60 per cent (.60 × 185). The product is 110. That will be your starting "training pulse rate." When your pulse has climbed to 110 and stayed there for longer than ten or twelve minutes, you will have tangible proof of the usefulness of running to your cardiovascular system.

The speed and power of your blood flow is the physiological measure of your success as a runner, and that is why checking your pulse is important. Slowly, over the first eight or ten weeks of your program, you will increase the pulse from 60 per cent of 185 to 70 per cent, and finally 80–85 per cent. The latter figure represents peak performance and total fitness.

Pulse rate changes are the most vital signs of the benefit of running to you. But there are other, more obvious, indications—changes that are more noticeable to the people in your life. All runners, almost without exception, lose significant amounts of weight as a result of a daily running program. Among my patients, Dan, a twenty-five-year-old salesman, lost 30 pounds (180 to 150) over a twelve-week period; Peter, a thirty-two-year-old busi-

Revitalizing You

nessman, took off 100 pounds (and 18 inches from his waistline); Carol, a twenty-five-year-old secretary, lost 25 pounds—and I could go on indefinitely.

Running itself does not peel off the pounds. As you will see in Chapter Eight, it is running combined with an altered diet that performs the "miracle" of permanent weight reduction. The more you run—i.e., the more seriously you take your program of exercise—the less likely you will be to sabotage it with steady doses of fatty, preservative-loaded, empty-caloried foods. You will become much more conscious of what fuel you use to stoke your furnaces. Running will also make you stop and consider the body you are conditioning to provide you with a longer, healthier life.

Slowly you will notice that your eating habits are changing. You will become aware of calories, preservatives, fat content, and sheer excess. At the same time, you will probably begin to notice that your sleeping habits are also changing. I do not mean that you will join the "early to bed, early to rise" club, but you will tend to fall asleep faster and sleep more soundly. Running is a fine outlet for the factors that interfere with sleep—tension, anxiety, and stress. (Vigorous non-competitive exercise thus relieves two of our most necessary physical activities—heartbeat and sleep—of the overloads that tend to impair their functioning.)

Stress cannot be avoided in a competitive, crowded culture. We are battered and worn and torn down by the process of life in modern American society. To combat the effects of keeping schedules, meeting deadlines, getting ahead, etc., the body must use energy. The body has on hand a reservoir of what Dr. Hans Selye calls "adaptive energy" (plus an emergency reserve) which is available for the normal daily ration of "battering." If the doses of stress become too heavy, the individual often experiences sudden drops in performance, drastic weight changes, disturbed sleep, anxiety, irritability, etc.—in other words, difficulty in coping with life.

Dr. Selye, who has spent many decades studying the phenomenon of stress, believes that adaptive energy is like "a special kind of bank account which you can use by withdrawals but can't increase by deposits." It is my belief, fortified by observation and experience, that jogging works to halt or slow down a "run" on your adaptive energy bank. The time you spend running is time away from the worries and demands of your normal environment. It is, in addition, time spent in building up your own sense of discipline and strength. The schedule or deadline has not disappeared while you have been out running, but your attitude toward it—your perspective on it—has altered. You thus need a smaller withdrawal from your energy account to deal with it—and the stress overload is avoided.

Not only does running help relieve stress and anxiety, it also helps one to throw away the crutches that sustained (and symbolized) the non-running tension sufferer. Running helps a person stop excessive smoking and drinking. Only a very tiny minority of my runner-patients continue to smoke after they have entered my program. The demands of daily jogging and the transformed life-style and mind-set of the runner are simply incompatible with smoking. You cannot have bad lungs—and be that negligent of your body—and be a runner.

Quite early on in the program the running starts to substitute itself as a replacement for smoking in a person's life: It relieves the tension that many experts feel is strongly related to the need to smoke (and drink). Daily jogging frees one from stress, but unlike smoking and drinking, it is a release that creates and demands peak physical fitness. The shortness of breath which the smoking habit induces in the beginning runner is so uncomfortable that it quickly becomes clear something must give—the bad habit or the good. Some periodically attempt to regain the nicotine habit, but quickly discover (again) that they cannot smoke and maintain their running program.

What I have said for smoking holds true for drinking alcohol except that the interference of moderate drinking with running is not nearly so great as smoking. Therefore you may well wish to continue imbibing temperate amounts of liquor even after you are a jogger. As we saw in the case of my patient Jerry, heavy boozing and running are not compatible, and I've seen a number of cases like Jerry's where the negative addiction was exchanged for the positive.

A final factor not mentioned above in the list of elements bearing directly on heart disease, but which obviously bears upon a person's accessibility to heart (or any other kind of) failure, is the *aging process* itself. A great deal of research has shown that while a person's chronological age is invariable, his physiological (not to mention psychological) age is capable of wide divergences from the chronological. In other words, it is possible—these days, even frequent—for a young man to burn himself out physically through drugs and alcohol usage so that, although chronologically in his late teens or early twenties, he looks, feels, and internally functions as if he were a man in his mid-thirties.

Similarly, however, it is equally possible for a woman in her chronological thirties, forties, fifties, or sixties to look, feel, and function as if she were ten to twenty years younger than she actually is! Anyone who has spent any time at all in the world of addicted runners has met dozens and dozens of middle-aged and elderly people whose physique, stamina, and physiology are living rebukes to one's own, even though you're twenty or thirty chronological years younger.

It's an object lesson in humility, frankly, to watch such people; but it's also an inspiration to you to see realized human potential in action. It also accounts for a peculiar psychological trait of runners—not only are they not afraid of growing older, many, many of them positively yearn to do so, partly because as they continue running, the effect on their bodies is to make them physiologically stronger and younger (in other words, *as time passes, they get younger!*), and partly because of the accumulated wisdom and self-sufficiency which years of running brings.

There are other exercises besides running that can do similar things for you. Bicycling, swimming, and rowing would be three. But none of them has the capacity running does to do so many things at once for a person's body, mind, and spirit. In terms simply of pulse rate and stroke volume of the heart, these exercises, particularly bicycling, are very close (but not even) with daily jogging. In terms of building up muscle tone and strength, swimming even has a slight advantage over running while bicycling and rowing are about even. For one thing, though, these other exercises are less readily available to most people than running. And for another more important reason, running is much better because it permits psychological and spiritual changes (in addition to the physical) which these other exercises have not been shown to do.

Chapter Five

PSYCHOLOGICAL BENEFITS

Every day after the first three or four weeks of your running program that you actually kick yourself out of bed (or pull yourself out of the armchair), put on your jogging shoes and gym shorts, and take your daily run, you are increasing your psychological and physical dependency on running. You are slowly becoming an "addict." Brace yourself, because gradually your "need" for running will become a profoundly important part of your whole identity.

If you throw yourself into it to the point of becoming positively addicted, running can dramatically change your body. It can even more dramatically and lastingly change your self-image, your sense of who you are and what you can do. Indeed, for the physical improvements to occur on a permanent basis, the quality of your life has to be changed as well. As this chapter will demonstrate, daily running leads you to a series of choices and decisions (many of which you will make unconsciously) that will alter your identity. The words may seem a bit unreal to you at this early point in your jogging career, as if I am describing some advanced, mysterious realm to which you will never gain access. Not so. I am talking about the next four to six months of your life.

That was precisely the amount of time it took my

friend Steve to overcome thirty-one years of sedentary ways and a downright aggressive suspicion of all things physical (save pushing himself away from his desk or the dining room table) and run in—and complete—a marathon in under four hours. At the post-run celebration, it was not the nine-minute-per-mile pace, nor the slim, tanned, and trim body at which his very old friends marveled. The real turnabout had occurred in Steve's mind, personality, and spirit; the physical acquisitions were reflections of a profound change in the way Steve thought about himself and presented himself.

Daily running had eroded and then erased Steve's lifelong feeling that a huge gap existed between the complex of things called mind/personality/emotions/spirit, on the one hand, and that physical extension and vehicle called the body, on the other. Most of you probably accept, albeit implicitly, this separation. As a result, you have neglected your physical body for a long time now (even if you were active in high school or college). This is a common situation for most people once they get out into the world and have to earn a living, raise a family, sink roots into the community, etc.

Less common, but equally detrimental, are those people devoted to the point of fetishism to physical appearance. The important point to make is that neither kind of person really has the best of either world, the physical or the non-physical, because he or she is making the mistake of cutting himself or herself off from an *equally* important realm of health. Mind and body are two integral parts of one existent whole; tremendous benefits derive to those who see them and treat them as such.

A renaissance of the ancient belief in a mind/body duality—i.e., a remelding of the mind/body split that has

Psychological Benefits

typified our thinking for far too long—leads us to an expanded notion of what health is. Regular running bridges the gap and shows you the potential that lies buried in your body, mind, heart, and spirit. Running regularly alters your former idea of what it is to be healthy.

For too long, medical doctors and laymen alike have accepted the traditional formula that health means the absence of disease. This purely negative understanding of a broad notion (health) must be surrendered for something that better evokes a fuller range of physical/mental/emotional/spiritual possibilities. As the life of running slowly becomes your way of life, your renewed sense of your bodily parts and the inter-connection of their potential will change, as will your outlook on what you accept as health. You won't be satisfied simply with the absence of disease. Running will indeed protect you, even immunize you, against a whole roster of chronic and acute ailments and diseases. Running will also free you for new appreciations and expectations from life. It will give you a positive task and means of contributing to your well-being.

The figurative distance you can run from your old ways of thinking about and presenting yourself will be illustrated by the disbelieving head-shaking and reminiscences Steve touched off in his old friends. "Is this that severe intellectual, fifty pounds overweight and scornful of anything more athletic than whistling in the shower?" queried an old college chum.

"My strongest, most recurrent memory of Steve," said he, "was of a day in our gym class at Colgate when the instructor, angry with us for our general sloth, ordered the entire class to run two laps of the quarter-mile track. A few of the guys raced to the front and breezed home barely perspiring. Most of us, though, dragged our tobacco-infested lungs and corpulent butts around the oval praying we would reach the finish line before vertigo set in.

"The main group of us were sullen, but silent as we ran. Steve, however, could hardly contain his rage. He wasted far more breath howling insults and invective at the instructor for inflicting this senseless and vulgar punishment than he did on running. Finally, gasping and red-faced, Steve fell over the finish line, swearing to himself and all the rest of us, 'I swear to God, no one will ever make me run another step in my life.'"

He was correct. No one could have. Once *he* made himself run, however, he gradually came to "burn" to run, because his daily running not only burned up calories, pounds, and cholesterol—it also incinerated the mental refuse of sloth, low self-esteem, fatigue, and listlessness. Steve learned, as you will learn readily enough, that one cannot be a runner and still retain a low sense of autonomy, independence, self-esteem, and personal productivity. The process of burning up the old ways of thinking, being, and acting occurs as soon as you become disciplined in your daily running, and it occurs in recognizable phases.

PHASE 1: A SURGE OF DEEP SATISFACTION

You are just getting started in your program of exercise and scheduled running. Although you may not notice it for a while, you have already begun to reap some early, non-physical benefits. For one thing, the very act of leaving the house and completing the marked-out distance gives you a sense of accomplishment and attainment. No

Psychological Benefits

matter what else has happened, you have survived. Running a mile is a damn hard thing to do for one who has not practiced it regularly. The daily completion of a mile run is a hard-won victory which produces deserved pride in oneself.

For another thing, running provides you with solitude: time away from other worries, agitations, and distractions. Especially at first, running will be hard for you, so you will have to concentrate on it with all your attention and put all your strength and energy into the heretofore accepted process of simple motion. This increased effort will, of necessity, force you to leave other things behind. Though you may not appreciate it while you are struggling through those eternal first miles, this detached perspective will become, in later phases, an enduring and sought after feeling.

Once you are two or three weeks into the program, the first spark of achievement will have turned into a steady flame. You have "discovered" a form of daily success, the heightening of which belongs to you alone. The complex and demanding aspects of adult life oftentimes block off the sources of palpable daily success. Job, family, relationships with people can drag on, become routinized, become "complicated," and provide only intermittent bursts of satisfaction between long periods of plodding, routine, or even defeat and problems. Frequently we feel that we are not in control of the vicissitudes.

You are in control of your running. And this sense of control—the sense of autonomy you feel as you jog through the park with no one at your back or on top of you—permeates into the other areas of your life. Part of the feeling of success and achievement provided by daily running is precisely the thought, "I've done it myself! I've shown the willpower. I intended to do something hard, and I did something hard, and by God, I'll do it again tomorrow."

This sort of feeling, common to every beginning runner, isn't often provided by our jobs and lives—at least not on a regular, dependable basis. More often we feel like Geraldine or Vilas (in Chapter One): helpless before our weight problems, our despondency, etc. For them, as for you, the very act of deciding to run is an assertion of will which put them (and you) back on the path to self-control. I know from my own life how important it is to feel that I have done something important on my own. The incentive and the accomplishment are yours alone—no one else's.

The decision to run—to act—reflects an effort to reassert control, to make use of our bodily powers as a tool—a natural tool—for our spiritual and intellectual rebirth. Phase 1, then, provides a new perspective based on a decision you made, on action you initiated, on a perpetuation you orchestrated.

PHASE 2: A SURGE OF LASTING PRIDE

Now you're running on a regular basis. It is the fifth or sixth week of your program, and you are running twenty to thirty minutes a day (2–3.5 miles). You have begun to witness the pounds falling away, to register firmed-up flesh, lowered pulse, a decreased cholesterol count. (The scale of heart-rate increase while running has become second nature to you.) In sum, you are getting used to being with your body, thinking about it, watching it respond to your new activity, working in concert with it. Autonomy

It's a beautiful morning: Dr. Art Mollen, Peggy Mollen, and members of the Arizona Marathon Society embark on a 6 A.M. run.

Bend at the waist and allow your trunk to hang parallel with the ground. Do not "bounce"—simply hang over and count slowly to 20.

Stand straight, arms at your sides. Slide your left hand down toward your knee and bring your right hand up until you feel the stretch on your right side. Do 20 side stretches.

Standing with your toes balanced on the edge of a step (as if you were going to do a back sommersault dive), push up and down on your toes with the arches and heels of your feet hanging in space. Do about 30 of these, up and down.

Place your left leg in front of you with the sole of your right foot touching the inside of your left upper leg. Then reach forward and grab your left foot with your hands; hold and count to 20.

Sitting with the soles of your feet together in front of you, push gently down toward the ground, holding your feet in your hands. Hold this position for about a count of 20.

Stay in the same position and lower your head as far **toward** your feet as you can, for a count of 10.

Don't run faster than you can comfortably hold a conversation with another runner.

Psychological Benefits

and health are now words with different meanings. Fitness is a new habit.

Most people will "wear" this new habit—that is, they will exude the pride and excitement (even euphoria) that comes from the purely cosmetic changes daily running produces. The loss of weight and inches on hips and waist, the improved muscle tone and diminished "droop" —in sum, the incredible youthfulness of your appearance, the increased feelings of athletic fitness and sexiness—will wash over most of you like a huge wave of joy. All of a sudden, the scale in your bathroom and the mirror in your bedroom will become pals and supporters, not enemies. They will no longer be seen as terrors lurking in the shadows.

Pride of appearance will be accompanied by pride of improved athletic condition, which will allow you to play extra sets of tennis or holes of golf (or whatever) without breathlessness or debilitating fatigue.

Clothes will cease to be a means of camouflaging a thing (your body) of which you are leery, and will instead become a means of enhancing its attractiveness. You will experience pleasure in purchasing new clothes or having the old ones taken in. This, too, is an accomplishment of Phase 2.

You will feel more attractive and present yourself more attractively. The increased sexual appeal of runners is evident; the "scientific proof" of their increased sexual potency, however, remains to be published. Yet my patients and runner friends assure me that regular running has upgraded their sexual performance. Their certainty on this point is matched only by their uncertainty as to whether the roots of the change are physical, psychical, or mystical.

By the end of Phase 2 you will be reveling in a whole raft of new-found attitudes and potentials stemming from physical changes, not to mention the gains of Phase 1 (sense of achievement, autonomy, health, etc.). In spite of having scaled these two plateaus, though, you will still have a sense of being your old self with new traits and capacities. As the weeks go by and you begin to get used to your new gifts, you will gradually free yourself of them (without losing them) and undergo the final transformation into something of a new person altogether.

PHASE 3: A SURGE OF INTANGIBLE MEANING

As the excitement of Phases 1 and 2 accomplishments gradually hardens into quiet confidence about their permanence, and as you gradually integrate these new "friends" into your ongoing patterns of thinking, acting, and talking, you will find yourself more and more open to new challenges and possibilities. At first you may experience these new frontiers as a feeling of nonchalance—"Aw gee, what's the big deal about running? I've got it all now." This is just a smokescreen. In a way, maybe it is the final defense of your old self, struggling to hang onto control of your life. For now, as you keep up the running and gradually increase it (perhaps you will now be doing from five to ten miles a day, or more), great underlying, "seismic" changes will be taking place in your identity. Phase 3 is the high plateau on which you will remain as long as you continue to run. Again I repeat: The mind/body duality is now overcome; the pleasure of new-found youthfulness, stamina, weight loss, health, increased athletic and sexual capacities is behind you; the feelings of

Psychological Benefits

achievement, of autonomy, of willpower are safe in your pocket.

Let them go! That's right, I said, "Let them go!" I do not mean literally, of course—how could you literally lose them if you continue to run?—but, rather, let them go psychologically so that you are no longer obsessed by them. The obsession may be fun, but it closes you off to the deeper meanings and satisfactions that lie above and beyond material and terrestrial gains. For something radically new to happen, something old must go out of being. The old you—despite the gains in confidence and appearance and health—must finally let go. Phase 3 running will make this happen.

The first sign you have of ascending the Phase 3 plateau may well be, believe it or not, a strange inability to answer the usual question posed by non-runners, "Why do you do it?" You will no longer feel entirely comfortable or sincere in simply spouting off a check list of specific physical and psychological benefits. Indeed, they may seem irrelevant or even beside the point.

You will, rather, answer in one of two ways—both of which carry the same meaning, "I run because I like it," or, "I feel empty when I don't run regularly." Both answers contain within them the kernel of the profoundly different type of life—infusing quality which occurs when you enter Phase 3 of running. In Phases 1 and 2 you were your old self with new and wonderful attributes. Now you are something of a new person. This is directly attributable to the purely physical activity of regular running. You now can directly experience the powerful mind-, spirit-, emotion-affecting correlates that purely physical activities produce. The result is that you, a person now running thirty to sixty minutes a day, are a very different person from the one who started to read this book.

The Phase 3 runner becomes, in the words of the psychiatrist William Glasser (author of *Positive Addiction*, a path-breaking book on the subject), "positively addicted." The runner experiences "a daily euphoria," a sense of wholeness, of relatedness with the world, of cleansing and cleanliness. Phase 3 runners feel rejuvenated by their daily runs; they feel it infusing the rest of the tasks they do with more energy.

Conversely, Dr. Glasser found that to miss a run creates discomfort, a sense of longing, even mourning. It is as if something important has been taken from the runner. Whatever the obstacle, however important the distraction, Phase 3 runners experience anxiety when the time for their daily run approaches and they are nowhere near their running gear or a course. They begin to plan out elaborate scenarios for alternate schemes. Some will run at midnight, if necessary. Others will grab fifteen minutes here, ten minutes there. Still others will contrive to run to accomplish their appointed rounds—to the library, to pick up their car from the service station, etc.

The Phase 3 runner has laid a foundation of confidence on which is built a framework of contemplation and realization of challenges. Within this phase there are plateaus of extended distances, increased rates of speed, and higher elevations. One of the most exciting challenges I have had highlighted a recent trip I made to Los Angeles. The campus of the University of California at Los Angeles is built on a series of hills. One of these hills runs along Sunset Boulevard and is nicknamed "The Hill." It is a long winding stretch—part of the two-mile circumference of the western part of the campus. I determined to do four laps. The first one I handled fairly easily, by the second one I was puffing. The third one was labored. As I came up to the fourth climb I took a series of deep breaths, set my will at its most determined notch, and started up. It was agony. But as the yards spun away under my feet and the summit loomed closer and closer a feeling of triumph and euphoria began to sweep over me. I had set myself a new challenge, and I had been equal to it.

A still higher realm of Phase 3 exists, however; a kingdom that might, at first blush, seem closed off to all but the most gifted and anointed. You marveled at those latter as they struggled into the Olympic Stadium in Montreal at the end of a 26-mile 385-yard run: the marathoners. Seven months ago Steve thought he could as easily have flown to the moon as emulate Frank Shorter, Lasse Viren, and Phidippides. Yet Steve, through dedication and perseverance, achieved a level of involvement and commitment through running beyond anything he had ever experienced in any other endeavor. The marathon became the world in which he discovered a new self. The finish line was, he thought at the beginning, his goal, but by mile twenty-two, simply getting one foot in front of the other was *the* monumental achievement. It was then that Steve knew an intensity of such totality, that his accomplishment of those last few miles represented a self-expressiveness that transcended a lifetime of pats on the back, compliments, and A's, not to mention a half-year's worth of pride, satisfaction, autonomy, health, fitness, i.e., all the goals of Phases 1 and 2.

Long before his aching body crossed the finish line under the four-hour barrier, Steve's awareness of the possible—of the potential in him and in his life—had so greatly expanded that he had achieved the ultimate realization which running brings: He was now a different person. The old limitations he had arbitrarily set for himself —I'm ugly, I'm lazy, I'm not an athlete, I'm not sexually appealing, etc., ad nauseum—had fallen away. He could, he now understood, be any and all of these things. The contours of his life had not drastically altered, but his perspective on its boundaries was much more vast.

But none of it was easy. *The only part of running that is easy* is stopping. Anyone can stop. To choose to continue, to choose to work hard mentally and physically, that is difficult, but it is the only way to reap meaningful rewards.

The reasons for the positive addiction and the negative feeling are simple: At the end of a good LSD run, you will not feel tired and lazy and eager to sink into an armchair for the remainder of the evening. You will want activity and meaningful intercourse, while non-runners will prefer rest, superficiality, artificial stimulants, etc. Time, the traditional enemy of the slothful, will become energized and productive for you—it will become a beckoning vehicle in which to do more and varied things.

The time you spend running will, in this phase, introduce you to the real meaning of the concept of relationship. Running is an activity that provides one with the experience of solitude—an activity that will assist you to know and value being alone. As you learn to relate to yourself, to allow your mind to roam and to dwell in areas relatively untouched before, you will come to appreciate the greater value of being with people and of sharing with them. Solitude, the relationship of you to yourself, becomes a meaningful experience when you run. This

Psychological Benefits

meaning can effect important changes in other parts of your life, because the spiritual and emotional lifts that jogging arouses do not disappear when you slow to a walk and head for home.

Chapter Six

PRACTICAL RUNNING

Here you are, just back from your first run (or, you blush to admit, still contemplating it), and I already have you breathing the heady air of Phase 3. In this chapter, therefore, I would like to bring you back to the practical aspects of running: selection of attire, recognition of injuries, finding time, running with people, and much more.

EQUIPMENT

I have found that the simple activity of buying running clothes and shoes can be very motivating for the beginner. Partly it is because most people love to buy new things, especially apparel; and partly it is because they know the shoes are "for real." You cannot do anything with a fine pair of jogging shoes except jog in them. They do not double as tennis sneakers or basketball shoes. So take special time out to equip yourself with the accoutrements of the art of jogging. A new sweat suit and bright-colored shoes will make you feel like a runner. (Just remember, though, that to *be* a runner, you must run.)

Make sure your running clothes feel comfortable and loose. In normal weather (spring, summer, and early fall), a cotton T-shirt and a pair of lightweight nylon or cotton trunks will do nicely. Obviously, something warmer, perhaps a sweat suit, is required in cold climates and during the winter. Trunks should not be too tight—you are not going to the beach in them. You do not want them to chafe against your inner thighs and irritate the skin.

Some people do not wear socks. Most world-class runners, for example, are highly conscious of the additional effort required to lift those few ounces of material again and again over the course of a long race. You, however, are not running against a pack of runners. On the other hand, if your shoe fits really well, and you like the feel of skin against nylon or leather, you can probably get away sockless. But most people prefer socks. As your running distance and time gradually increases, socks will be an insurance policy against blisters. Just make sure that they are smoothly fitted to your skin before you put your shoes on. Wrinkles in socks equal blisters and raw spots on feet. (Wool socks stay drier longer than cotton socks and thus chafe less in the course of a run.)

Shoe selection is of decisive importance. Those several centimeters of rubber sole are all that stand between the sole of your foot and a very hard surface. Anything other than the *right* pair of shoes can put you out of the running business permanently. With a poorly made shoe, or a badly fitted one, you risk far more than blisters; you risk feet, leg, and knee injuries. Let me repeat what I said in Chapter Two: Do not try and build a running career on tennis or basketball shoes. They do not have the flexibility and support that are mandatory in a running shoe.

In choosing a shoe, it is *your* needs and requirements—your bone structure, weight, etc.—that should be the determining factor—not what everyone else is wearing. The

Practical Running

more you weigh—hence the harder you will be pounding the ground—the greater the support and sole thickness you will need. If you have problems with your ankles or Achilles tendons, you will need a shoe with extra heel support. If you suffer from bone spurs or bruises or "jogger's heel," the shoe's heel-cupping properties should be stressed. Whatever your special requirement, all shoes must have enough room in the toe area so that your toes do not bang into the front of the shoe, damaging skin and toenails in the process.

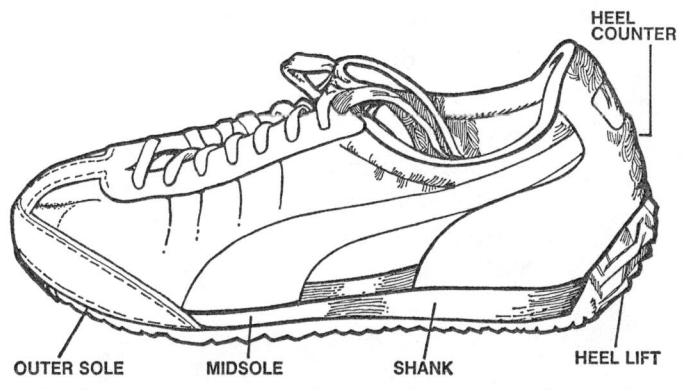

The basic components of a good running shoe: 1) a sturdy outersole; 2) about half an inch of midsole for cushioning; 3) a thick shank to elevate the heel; 4) a rolled, flared heel; and 5) a firm heel counter for support.

The key components of a successful jogging shoe are: 1) adequate heel support, 2) flexible sole, 3) good arch support both inside and out, 4) light weight (between 9 and 12 ounces). Most "official" shoe ratings (such as the recent one in *Runner's World*) are authored by serious runners for serious and semi-serious runners. Thus they tend to overemphasize light weight. The average runner needs a shoe that offers protection, support, and guaranteed shock-absorbing qualities. Consequently, a heavier shoe will more often fit the needs of my patients (on whose experience I base my ratings) than it will the requirements of professional runners. There are several good brands of jogging footwear, out of the literally dozens on the market, that provide the required snugness, comfort, and support, although the price of some of them will cause you to inhale sharply. The investment ($20 to $40), however, is a necessary and worthwhile one.

>   Pony Roadrunner
>   Nike Waffle Trainer
>   New Balance 320
>   Adidas Country
>   Adidas Runner
>   Brooks Vantage
>   Nike LD-1000
>   Adidas Formula One
>   Brooks Villanova
>   Adidas TRX
>   Converse World Class Trainer
>   Etonic Street Fighter
>   Puma Easyrider
>   Pony California
>   Adidas SL 76

Let me briefly discuss the qualities of some of the shoes I have just mentioned. The Nike Waffle Trainer is particularly well-suited for areas that are grassy or have frequent rain because they provide extra traction. The

Adidas Runner, because of its increased sole support, is recommended for concrete and asphalt running.

As you progress in your running program, be careful to note from time to time the condition of the heels of your footgear. Do not let them wear down or you will risk needless injury to your Achilles tendon or cause pains in your calf and knee. A run-down heel causes the foot to hit the ground unevenly and produces unaccustomed stress on the leg. Since in ten minutes of running your feet strike the ground approximately 1,700 times each, the slightest unevenness in the heel can rapidly result in problems.

FINDING THE TIME

The successful business people, socially active, and devoted family types among you have probably had little difficulty sandwiching your daily mile run in among your various activities. The five minutes of stretching exercises, the ten-minute run, and the ten- to fifteen-minute cooling-down and shower time have not seriously taxed your schedule. As your enjoyment increases and your need to continue challenging yourself grows, however, you may begin to experience some difficulty in finding a whole hour to devote to your running each day. There are various solutions to this dilemma.

The most radical, and the one I recommend, is to begin to rethink and reorder some of your heretofore sacred priorities. I do not mean divorce your wife, abandon your children, resign your job, or take up holy orders. I do mean that you should take a long, hard look at the way you spend your time. Most of us waste a good deal of time during the day in the space of ten- to twenty-minute blocks. Using these fractions to better advantage would give you the necessary running time.

There are some days, though, when appointments and obligations simply absorb all one's available time. If this happens on a regular but not everyday basis, you could run longer on the days when your schedule is lighter. That is, you would not run as often but still run as far. If the jammed-up days only occur episodically, you can split your running time. Arise a little earlier in the morning and do part of your run; then finish up when you get home in the evening.

RUNNING ALONE OR WITH PEOPLE

I believe that beginners need the support of other runners, of fellow-travelers, so to speak, on the road to Phase 3. This is not a discovery unique to jogging, of course. Every self-help program in the country from Weight Watchers to Gamblers Anonymous appreciates the benefits that accrue to a wavering novice from the pooled willpower and self-confidence of a group.

Therefore, if at all possible, I urge you to launch yourself on a running program with other people—husbands, wives, children, neighbors, friends, like-minded strangers. I even notice a number of people who run with their dogs. There are now hundreds of jogging societies around the country, spread out over nearly every one of the fifty states. There are also increasing numbers of fitness centers like my own in Phoenix. Runners are generally congenial folks, and the beginner, with a little bit of effort,

Practical Running

can find comrades with whom to start the Great Adventure.

Groups supply strength to the weary and faint of heart; they help cut through the excuses and alibis. Groups can thus sustain you . . . *for a while*. But I underscore these last three words because the commonest mistake beginning runners can make is to assume that the group will pull them along forever. A jogging society should be used like a lamp—for enlightenment, not support.

Thus, it is essential that each member of the running group be self-motivated, that he or she come to the group runs with the personal decision to run already made. A strong group is a collection of like-minded individuals who have committed themselves to acting on their decision to run. Be careful, though, of too many leaners and borrowers or your running bank will soon have more withdrawers than savers.

As you progress in speed and distance, however, the chances of finding people whose running pace and daily schedule coincides with your own diminishes. Unless, that is, you live in Eugene, Oregon, where, in a population of 90,000 there are nearly 10,000 daily joggers and many more occasional ones. For the average American runner, the only partner will be yourself. Though getting used to solitude may not be easy, the lesson, once learned, is invaluable in all areas of life. The kind of discipline and fulfillment that comes with fruitful solitude constitutes the granite base of human strength.

SECOND AND THIRD WIND

The folklore of running contains no more sacred tale than that of the "second" and "third" wind. As with most learned traditions of this type, the documentation or scientific validation is scant; but every runner "knows" they exist. In fact, many runners "wait" for them as small children wait for their favorite television program. Second and third winds represent a feeling of vigor, a feeling of enthusiasm, a bounteous charge of energy that sweeps over your body just at the point when you have decided to stop running and begin again some other day. They may be more psychological than physical, but the feeling of revitalization that they bring is palpable.

In my experience, a second wind usually occurs after about five or ten minutes (or one mile). It represents the runner's capacity to experience an increased amount of endurance. Usually it is coterminous with the first signs of perspiration. The increased amount of endurance we feel stems from our bodies' successful adaptation to the increased amount of stress we are putting on it; the perspiration is a signal that our inner homeostatic mechanisms have adapted to the outer environment in which we are running. Rather than meaning that an increased amount of oxygen has mysteriously entered your lungs and been distributed throughout your body, second wind is the feeling you get when your body has completed its adjustment to the running and the environment of the run.

The third wind is an experience reserved for those people who regularly run six to eight miles a day (fifty or sixty minutes). Normally, they are physically and spiritually fatigued when they approach the end of a day's run, but occasionally they are overcome by a tremendous burst of energy that makes them feel as if they could run on forever. While no one I know has managed to complete a run of that distance, many friends of mine have continued running for another thirty to sixty minutes on this auxiliary source of power. The third wind is part psychological (you happen to be feeling really good that day; it is a bright sunny day; you have nothing special or pressing to do when you get home) and partly physical (you have probably been holding back a good deal of energy; you have reached a plateau in your conditioning that permits you to ask more of your body than you knew). Whatever the source, these renewals serve to spark us along on our appointed rounds. They become like old friends, running companions, as it were.

MINOR INJURIES

Runners are injured occasionally. The feet, after all, are striking the ground heavily and frequently for an extended period of time. There are two main causes of injuries: 1) attempting to cover too much distance too quickly; 2) some problems in the alignment of foot, knee, and hip; 3) improper shoe fit. On the next few pages I will describe some of the more common problems, their symptoms, and treatment.

Blisters: Blisters are caused by friction (heat) generated by poorly fitted shoes, worn shoes, or wrinkled or loose socks. If the blister is causing pain and pressure, it is a good idea to puncture it with a sterilized needle. Clean the area and use sterile gauze pads to remove the fluid.

Do not remove the skin from the blister. Cover the exposed area with a gauze pad, some padding (usually moleskin), and tape. This will allow you to continue running. Small blisters can be handled with an extra pair of socks, making sure that both pairs are clean and snug fitting. See a physician if the area becomes infected.

Achilles Tendinitis: The second most common form of injury, it usually results from sudden changes in running surface, shoe type, speed, or running style. The result is pain and stiffness during and after the run, with occasional swelling and difficulty bending the toes upward. Sometimes the soreness is so acute that running becomes impossible, and walking difficult.

If the stiffness is bearable, running on a flat, solid surface at a relaxed pace will usually solve the problem. More acute tendinitis requires ice packs on the Achilles tendon, stretching exercises, and perhaps heel lifts or orthotic supports to correct any biomechanical error or fault that may be present.

Chrondromalacia of the Knee: A common injury, the causes of which are not known. Basically, though, it is caused by overuse of the knee. The knee absorbs a great deal of the pounding as your feet strike the ground some 5,000 times in an hour. Sometimes, as a result of instability of the foot-ground strike over an extended period, the patella tendon begins to slip back and forth. The runner experiences pain and swelling. It can be treated by running on a flat surface at reduced speed, ice applications after running, and shoe supports or inserts.

Heel-bone Damage: Some runners develop inflammation of the bursa surrounding the area where the heel bone and the Achilles tendon come together. Others develop "spurs," bony growths around the bursa or fasca.

Heel pains should be attended to immediately, by inserting arch supports or donut-type pads in the shoe.

Leg and Foot Bursitis: Bursitis is caused by friction occurring when the tendon passes over the bone improperly. The pain and swelling associated with this injury can occur on or under the knee cap, between the groin muscle and the hip, on the bony prominence of the thigh just below the hip, on the heel, in the big toe. It can be corrected with proper padding in the shoe or a switch to a shoe better designed for your biomechanics.

Shin Splints: Pain and swelling in the lower leg caused by the anterior tibial muscle being pulled away from the bone. The cause of this injury often is an inflexible shoe which transmits the shock of running to the leg muscle rather than absorbing it. A more flexible shoe, stretching exercises, ice after running, a softer running surface, and, perhaps, heel lifts and orthotics can relieve this condition.

Leg-muscle Pulls: These are caused by improper warm-up or excessive speed work. A heating pad can relieve the pain; proper stretching exercises and a more moderate pace can prevent its recurrence.

Back Pain: People who have low back pains when they start a jogging program sometimes complain that the running exacerbates the problem. Initially, they may be right, but as they learn to enjoy the process and benefits of running, their need for excuses lessens and the pains disappear. I have found that 75 per cent of my patients who complain of low-back pain suffer from psychosomatic pain rather than from a structural defect in the back. Nervous tension can lead to muscle spasms in that area.

Fifteen per cent of sufferers from low-back pain, however, have one leg shorter than the other. A much smaller percentage have disc problems. Persistent pain should be reported to your doctor.

Low-back pain can be treated with heel lifts if the problem is disparity in leg length or stretching and strengthening exercises if the problem is with the muscles. Leg raises are recommended highly.

Muscle Cramps: Muscles "cramp" or knot up when a runner has allowed himself to become dehydrated. Dehydration is accompanied not only by excessive thirst, but the loss of copious amounts of electrolytes. Electrolytes are the main minerals in the tissues: salt, potassium, calcium, and magnesium. Cramps can be avoided by increased intake of fluids. Runners who work out regularly at midday or who live in warmer climates need to be especially conscious of possible dehydration.

Twisted Ankle: There is no need to describe the cause of this injury. Any of you who have ever stepped in a hole or on uneven ground or lost your footing recognize instantly the sharp pain and resultant tenderness of a sprained ankle. Immediate application of ice will hold down the swelling. An X ray should be taken as a precautionary measure. The only "cure" is rest.

I am sure you noticed that the basic theme of this section is not so much that injuries and infirmities occur, but rather that most injuries and infirmities need not seriously interfere with your running program. Any physical pain or discomfort should be immediately attended to and diagnosed, but except for sprains and bone breaks in the lower extremities, curtailed running is generally not the best prescription for the ailments discussed in this section. I will discuss the whole issue of "excuses" in the next chapter, but I want to caution you against using twinges, stitches, aches, etc., as grounds for returning to a sedentary existence. Medically speaking, there are no grounds for choosing that option.

GUIDELINES FOR ELDERLY JOGGERS:

Actually, these pointers are useful for all of us, but anyone over sixty needs to take special care to implement them.

1. Adequate fluid hydration: 8 oz. of water for every mile run.
2. No eating before walking or jogging.
3. Initial moderate fatigue is to be expected. You will probably need increased sleep for the first several weeks to aid your body in its adjustment to the new exercise regime.
4. Decrease your consumption of meats and increase your consumption of fruits and vegetables.
5. Increase your intake of vitamin C and iron.
6. Do not shirk or skimp your stretching exercises.
7. Always allow five minutes to warm up and five minutes to cool down.

ODDS AND ENDS

After you have been running for a few weeks, you will probably discover these (and other) small, but valuable, lessons:

If you are plagued by blisters, put on socks or take off the ones you have been wearing. (I know it seems primitive, but it works.)

If your heels or nipples are getting red and sore from chafing, put some vaseline around the inner heel of your shoes and over your nipples. Or use Band Aids.

Double tie your shoelaces . . . that is, unless you want an excuse for stopping, in which case don't double tie them.

Pin your keys to your shorts lest they fall out of your pocket and you end up having to walk home or climb in through a window.

Don't overdress. What you regard as cold weather at the beginning of a run becomes remarkably warm after a half mile. Go lightly attired in all but the coldest weather so you won't have to worry about how to dispose of unneeded garments in mid-run.

POSITIVE ADDICTION

In this last section of the chapter on the advanced art of joggery, I want to deal with the non-practical side of running, with the attainment of the ultimate goal: addiction or the *becoming* a runner. This new identity does "happen," but not all at once. You pass through stages in the art of joggery, but there is a greater likelihood of your reaching the final stage—the stage of a new identity—if you know what the goal is. The goal is "euphoria," but like any spiritual state (*nirvana* in Buddhism, *moksha* in Hinduism, etc.) one must work toward it. Like anything special and rare, euphoria takes times to occur. There is a lot of ground and effort between you and euphoria, between your first tentative strides and positive addiction.

Practical Running

Phase 1, the decision to start, was not too difficult. Obviously, it was the most important stage, but it was also the most commonplace one once you had made up your mind that your old habits were no longer acceptable. In Phase 2, the first few weeks, you were still caught up in the pleasure of this new event in your life and the results you were achieving with it. The running itself was still hard, but you were becoming increasingly accustomed to it.

In Phase 3, ten to twelve weeks into the program, you have approached the crucial juncture. You have achieved a lot of your original goals—e.g., weight loss, blood pressure and pulse decreases, an end to smoking. The program for which you may have signed up and paid money is approaching its conclusion; the runners in the group are splitting up and returning to their lives. The early excitement and novelty have worn off, and, frankly, it is getting harder and harder to drag yourself out of bed for the purpose of running.

Thus, Phase 3 is the Desert of the Devils—a place where you have run beyond the lush pastures of your original understanding, goals, and accomplishments. Now, if ever, is when running will seem a useless drudge because you have not yet found its true meaning. It will seem, indeed, as though there is no "true meaning," and so you may be tempted to stop before you have crossed the desert and found the paradise on the other side.

The drudgery or boredom that may overcome you in Phase 3 is like the shortness of breath and muscle strains of Phases 1 and 2—something you must run through. *Running is not something with a beginning, a middle, and an end.* It is a new way of life.

If you are reaching the critical juncture of Phase 3,

here are some practical tips to help you (though ultimately only you and your personal will can win this battle). Your disenchantment may stem from increased fatigue or muscle strain or "leadenness" in the legs. Frequently these occur because Phase 2 runners start to speed up the pace to increase their interest. Sometimes they speed up too much and begin to run on their toes like a sprinter. Both these alterations make it harder to run long distances with ease. So slow down your pace and return to the more comfortable heel-toe step. You may also have begun to cheat on your prerun "stretchies." If you do them carefully, however, you will ache less during and after the run, and if you ache less, the temptation to quit is more easily ignored.

So much for practical tips. The main point to emphasize for the man or woman who is running from Phase 3 into the last stage is this: Concentrate on changing your outlook. Make it into an *in*look, and your desire for running will begin to renew itself.

Chapter Seven

EXCUSES AND THEIR OVERCOMING

It has taken me quite a few years to find something that people will avoid more scrupulously than running, but in the course of preparing this book, I discovered such a thing: writing. The very morning I intended to begin this chapter on excuses, in fact, I received a telephone call from an author who said he really couldn't write today "because you know, Art, I've got to get in my ten miles or I'll never be in shape for the San Diego Marathon."

I was astonished that anybody would actually use running as a pretext to avoid doing something else. I would never have thought it possible because in the years I've been practicing medicine and motivating people to jog, I have waded knee-deep in a never-ending river—at times a flood—of excuses, rationalizations, pretexts, explanations, pleas, ex post factos, promises, apologies, vows, defenses, threats, cajolements, and exaggerations all aimed at one target: avoiding the daily run.

Excuses, I have learned, are as common as pollutants in our society and, like pollutants, are harmful human creations which humans can do something about. An excuse equals an evasion. The telltale signs of the excuse maker—the downcast look, the hesitant voice, the overly rehearsed soliloquy—all are manifest symptoms of a latent desire to avoid something.

Excuses come in all sizes and categories and shapes: physical, mental, spiritual, temporal, climatic, etc. In this chapter, I will illustrate some of the more common ones to aid you in recognizing and overcoming your own particular brand. I must, however, interject a cautionary note at this point: The decision to recognize and deal with an excuse five weeks into the running program is similar to the decision to recognize and deal with your lack of fitness before you even came to me. The decision to overcome excuses, like the decision to begin a running program, is yours alone. I could not have "talked" you into jogging, nor can I win an argument with someone who is bound and determined to excuse himself from running.

Argumentation and long-winded discussion are the excuse makers' home ground, anyway. They serve as a kind of briar patch where the excuse artist can elude the most dauntless pursuer. So I've learned over the years not to follow the Br'er Rabbits onto their turf. Instead, I follow the example of Alexander the Great who, when confronted with the Gordian Knot, simply raised his sword and cut through the tangle.

I listen to whatever my patients tell me about their physical ills. When the complaint has substance, I prescribe treatment. *I never excuse them,* however. The decision to run or not to run must be theirs alone. In fact, I tell my patients right from the start that their excuses will not work on me, that I know them all anyway, having heard them a hundred times. So, I inform them, why waste your breath unless, maybe, you have a rare excuse specimen I have not heard and could add to my collection?

I have said it before, and I will surely say it again—running isn't easy. In the beginning, especially, it may hurt—

Excuses and Their Overcoming

and I don't mean the physical stress so much (though this is not irrelevant) as the discombobulation that daily jogging causes in our usual agendas of sloth, indulgence, and appointments. It's so easy in our society to just sit back and take a snooze or sip a martini or flick on the TV set. We have far fewer cultural agencies or incentives that urge us to exert ourselves physically. As a nation, we love sports, of course, but largely as spectators watching the kids or the pros. We may have been high school or college athletes, but now we're lucky if we play golf or tennis once a week. That's not fitness. Running, daily running, will create fitness, but the process isn't easy, and it entails a certain amount of pain and change. Hence the excuses.

A French philosopher once said that hypocrisy is the homage vice pays to virtue. Well I have learned that excuses are the homage the lazy pay to the fit. Excusers aren't down on running. In their hearts they are usually quite convinced that running is good for them, but they're afraid of a little bit of pain and a lot of change, and they're guiltily attached to a life of self-indulgence, so they invest a lot of energy into dreaming up rationalizations that convince them that although they'd like very much to be healthy and fit, they simply cannot do so right now because they're not healthy or fit enough. Excuses don't really fool anyone, least of all the excuser, but they make him feel better and they hide the truth in a lot of verbal whipped cream. Herewith are some of the varieties.

HO-HUM ANOTHER BORING RUN

Practically everyone who has begun to run has been tempted to stop running by an attack of tedium. The virile grandpappy of all excuses for storing away the Adidas is boredom. It is a high arid plateau over which all runners have to pass before they learn to enjoy running and to welcome the time away it provides.

Those who have confronted and overcome boredom have been able to honestly admit to themselves that this was not a new feeling which jogging introduced into their lives. We do not live in a society where solitude and self-amusement are highly regarded capacities. On the contrary, we are used to doing everything with other people, to being entertained, scheduled, amused, programmed, provided for. When, in addition, we must subject our overindulged bodies to regular stress—jogging, with its concommitant aches, pains, sweat, etc.—the reaction of the mind is . . . boredom.

Boredom is apathy's most staunch defender.

There is no pat answer to the excuse of boredom, just as there are few answers to any of the excuses we dream up to postpone or reject what is good for us. You have to run through your boredom, that's all. You may even want to look upon the time alone with yourself, which running provides, as an opportunity for thought, reflection, prayer, pipe-dreaming, or mental voiding. In any event, if you stick to your jogging for ten to twelve minutes every day over the course of three or four months, and if you don't run too fast, and if you try to arrange to run in the company of other runners, then the boredom will be marginal, and more importantly, it will gradually start to be replaced by your increasing aptitude for solitude, reflection, self-amusement.

By the time you are addicted to running—somewhere in the fourth or fifth month—boredom will start to be seen for the defense and the rationale that it is. You may even come to agree with the author Thomas Wolfe when he wrote that "life isn't dull, but sometimes people are small." So my final advice about boredom is this: Confront it head on; see if you can tie it in with other reactions you have in life; see if you can figure out what it means and what it is camouflaging.

GEE, DOC, IT HURTS

Herb, forty-three, a clothing salesman, walks into my office once a week with his regular Thursday meek look. It means he has not run the previous day or two. Herb smiles wanly, assumes his most humble posture, breathes deeply, and launches into his circumlocution.

"Art, I've got this awful blister on my heel." A pause where I am expected to commiserate.

"It really hurts, Doc, no kiddin'," he insists when I say nothing. "I got it four days ago at our Monday run, and I haven't been able to do another mile since."

"Well, Herb, we all go through these early tribulations in our running careers. You've simply got to run through things like blisters. After the first mile you won't even feel them. And more to the point, if your shoes fit properly, you won't get blisters."

Herb has heard all this before so he is not slowed so much as a millisecond by my elucidation of calm truth. Even while I am talking, he has been mobilizing his troops for another assault, which he launches scarcely before the last sentence is off my lips.

"Oh, but Doc, the blisters ain't nothing compared to this pain in my side. Do you know what pain is, Doc? I mean *real* pain? It feels like a silken thread tightening in my gut—" Herb now clutches his side, undoubtedly fancying himself a wounded John Wayne on the slopes of Mt. Iwo Jima, passion matched only by rhetoric, "Every time I move it stabs like a blade. It radiates all over my innards. I feel like my kidney is falling out and my colon is twisting like taffy—"

I break in before Herb passes out. "Fine, Herb, I get the picture. You're suffering from a stitch in your side. We all get them occasionally. I've already told the group what to do about stitches. Use your palm or your fingertips to put pressure on the afflicted area while you run. Bear down hard, and keep running. It will disappear."

Herb reflects on this familiar advice a second or two while the wheels turn in his resourceful brain. "Yeah, okay, I know that, Doc, and I do what you say, but it doesn't help with this ache in my calf. It feels like a terrible tightness which increases with every step I take until I can hardly put one foot in front of the other. But there is no way I can apply my palm or fingertips to my calf."

Herb is really trotting out the old stand-bys. "Now c'mon, Herb, we dealt with muscle cramps in our first lesson. You know perfectly well that you should stop running and stretch your calf muscles by standing on a step, backward, lifting up and down slowly using your toes."

Finally there is silence in the room. His initial sortie repulsed, Herb is momentarily bested but still undaunted. Excuses are now multiplying like rabbits in his brain. Eventually he hauls out the big one. I sit quietly knowing what stratagem is about to be unlimbered.

"Well, Dr. Mollen, I didn't want to mention this because I don't want to scare you or scare me either, for that matter. But I've been having pains right here." He proceeds to thump portentously the anterior chest wall

Excuses and Their Overcoming

behind which his stout heart is pulsing away at its usual 84 beats per minute. "It's a sharp pain, and sometimes it stretches all the way down to my stomach and up to my head." There is a studied, deathlike pause while he delivers the *pièce de résistance* which he undoubtedly picked up the night before watching "Marcus Welby" reruns. "I can even feel it like a ball of fire in my left armpit."

Medical vocabulary failing me at this point, I say to him, "Bull, Herb, pure, unadulterated bull."

Lest you think me heartless or incompetent, I should point out that I have carefully monitored Herb's heart for the two months he has been in the running program and I am intimately acquainted with his medical history. I have given him two stress-EKG tests in that two-month period, and I have examined his heart three times a week. The chance that Herb is experiencing anything even remotely resembling a legitimate cardiac event is about as likely as an epidemic of priapism in a convalescent home.

If boredom is the patriarch of the clan of non-jogging excuses, hypochondria is the king's closest blood relation. Here, too, the "honest" complainer will be forced to admit that these imaginary ailments are a well-oiled means of avoiding all manner of difficult or seemingly unpleasant tasks in his or her life. As Herb (or you) continues to run, the excuses will ring hollower and hollower, and eventually will be heard no more in the land. For pain, for boredom—for every excuse not to run—the solution is . . . running.

BUSY, BUSY, BUSY

Arthur rises at five each morning in order to be at the office by 6:30, and he does not stagger home until 10:30 each night. He grabs a sandwich at his desk, rarely has time to eat dinner, sits on every board of directors, sponsors every charity in town, does not know what a vacation is, barely recognizes his own children, and has not seen the tops of his shoes in almost a decade.

As I was figuring out my approach to this seemingly unassailable bastion, I could not overcome my amazement that at a time when our civilization is setting unheard of records for the creation of leisure time, the Arthurs of this world barely have opportunities for unharassed bowel movements, let alone daily jogging. Since each item on the schedule had a "natural" defense perimeter, I had to undermine the entire edifice. "Arthur," I inquired, "what good is a work schedule that destroys your health and your fitness?"

"You are right, Doctor, but what can I do?"

Here again I had to avoid the particulars. If I said, "Come home earlier from work," for example, he would reply, "But if I don't get these sales reports ready for tomorrow, my staff will sit around and I will lose money." Instead I told him, as I would tell any of you with similarly crowded schedules, you must decide what is important, what must take priority. Having done that, you will then find a place and a time for running.

Arthur looked again at the test results, peered at his bulging waistline, and remembered that there was a YMCA down the street from his office. He also "found" some time which was free. Now, every weekday at noon, Arthur can be found on the running track of the YMCA, pounding out his mile.

THE LONELINESS OF THE LONG, SLOW DISTANCE

Peggy, thirty-three, has no difficulty making it to our group runs on Monday, Wednesday, and Friday mornings. Tuesday, Thursday, Saturday, and Sunday, however, are another matter. When the herd instinct is not there to support her, she cannot be depended upon to do her prescribed jogging. "I know running is good for me, but I just cannot seem to get up the gumption to run by myself," she regularly informs me.

As I've said, it is usually treacherous to follow up a statement like Peggy's with the obvious question, "Well, why not?" because it thereby opens a verbal tap that may flood the room with rationalizations. For illustrative purposes, however, I will pose the question to Peggy and let her go on for a minute or two. Her brand of excuse is "instructional," as they used to say in medical school about cases of beriberi.

"Really, Peg? Why not?"

"Well, I don't have anyone to run with. My husband won't get out of bed early enough, my neighbors think I'm crazy, and so do my children. And when I run alone, men stop their cars and honk their horns at me, or kids yell names, or dogs chase me. God, Doc, I'm afraid I might get molested or raped."

We'll stop the soliloquy at this point. So far Peg is doing a good job of buck passing. In effect, she's saying, "It's not my fault, not *my* decision, that I don't run. It's *theirs*—kids, dogs, neighbors, strangers, etc. I'm just the innocent victim." Peggy is doing what a lot of crafty excusers do: She is dodging responsibility for her decision not to run. Dodging responsibility is a peculiar characteristic of the halfway excusers. Even when they run, it is in large groups, as if even then they need the reassurance and mutual sharing of responsibility that large groups appear to give.

I am told by my friends and colleagues in psychiatry and psychology that the main key these days to helping people get over mental problems is to get them to own up, to take responsibility, for much of what is going wrong in their lives. I gather that this process is a hard one to initiate because people cling to their defenses and pretenses, especially buck passing. Well, I just want to report from my seemingly distant field of medical/health care that I am encountering the same sort of responsibility dodging as the psychotherapists. I have learned that the only sure way of getting somebody hooked onto LSD (Long Slow Distance) running is to teach them *to take responsibility for making the decision to run.* Only then can excuses be seen in their true light. In fact, I am seriously thinking of having all the beginners on my running program sign (and repeat daily) a statement to the effect, "I choose to run today, and if I do not run, it is because I choose not to."

RUNNING IS INJURIOUS TO MY HEALTH

Once in a very great while an excuse really will require extended discussion. Peggy had a friend, Sue, who used to run in our group. She was a dependable jogger for a time,

Excuses and Their Overcoming

and then inexplicably one day she dropped out and never came back. I learned from Peggy what Sue's excuse was. She had met a doctor at a cocktail party—a rotund giant of a man with a red face and a large cigar in his mouth—who had pooh-poohed jogging at first, and then, when Sue defended it, had come on in his best professional manner with a lot of phoney gobbledygook doctors often use to impress, confuse, terrify, and mislead laymen.

"My dear," said he, "if your body continues to sustain the constant surface shock of long-distance running, you'll suffer debilitating consequences to your kidneys, breasts, and uterus. The ligamentous tissue of the breast and uterus will be weakened with resultant sagging and displacement. Furthermore, renal malfunctions such as hematuria are a risk for you." He then proceeded to cite what poor Sue thought to be a long list of scientific papers reporting experiments that proved his point.

Since excuses are after-the-fact decisions made for other reasons, it is usually dangerous to get bogged down into refuting them—as we saw. But in certain instances, such as this one where a woman was genuinely frightened away from running by the irresponsible words of a physician, it is important to reply to an excuse.

The first thing to say is this: There is absolutely no documented evidence whatever to validate any of the points the doctor thinks he has scored. On the contrary what evidence exists points strongly to the opposite conclusion: Joggers, despite occasional aches and muscle injuries, show a markedly *reduced* incidence of internal malfunctions. Dr. Jack Scaff, who has conducted many surveys on the runners in his Honolulu Marathon Clinic, has found a greatly reduced susceptibility among runners to gastrointestinal problems—e.g., ulcers, diverticulitis, colitis, hemorrhoids, etc.

Dr. Joan Ullyot, a respected sports medicine physician and author of several fine books on jogging for women, has studied extensively the effects of running on the female anatomy and physiology. Contrary to a prevailing prejudice about "sagging and displacement," Ullyot's work indicates that the proper running program enhances the tone and definition of the musculature of a woman's chest and pelvis, thereby stabilizing breasts and pelvis.

I've cited only two researchers who have studied the effects of jogging on the body and its fitness. There are many others—Bassler, Sheehan, Morehouse, Cooper, Kostrubala, Cavanaugh, etc.—whose findings, while not yet definitive or systematic, clearly point to the conclusion that jogging, when performed according to a sound program, is one of the very best means available to human beings to create fitness and well-being.

The so-called jogger's diseases (low-back pains, vericose veins, injuries of the knee, ankle, foot, etc.) which have been written about somewhat breathlessly in the popular press are half-truths blown into indictments by people, like Sue's doctor friend, who know nothing about jogging and who have not studied the literature. In truth, runners are obviously more prone to injuries of the leg and the foot than the person who doesn't run, in much the same way that a deer hunter is more likely to accidentally shoot himself than the man who never leaves his armchair. But in both instances (the runner and the hunter), if proper preparation and caution are employed, the risk is tiny and well worth the benefits.

It is, in any case, extremely rare for someone to suffer a coronary while running. The majority of heart attacks occur between 9 P.M. and 6 A.M., when people are sedentary. When something of this nature does happen to a runner while he or she is running, there is nearly always a special explanation—e.g., the runner had a history of cardiac disease and he had not been stress-tested to discover his maximum tolerance for violent exercise.

At the risk of antagonizing many of my colleagues across the country, most doctors practicing in the United States are used to treating illness; they know very little about health, its components, and its creation. Questions of diet, fitness, exercise, and human-performance physiology do not fall in the province of the average physician, but unfortunately, this does not seem to prevent many of them from pontificating like oracles about such things.

In general, therefore, I advise my patients, friends, and fellow runners to beware of the advice, barbs, jibes, and prejudices of non-joggers, even ones with M.D. gracing their names. Runners often take a lot of heat from non-runners, but in 95 per cent of the cases, the critics are overweight, sedentary people in search of a rationale not to exercise and are, therefore, threatened by people who do. Runners are living reproaches to non-runners, and the latter often count it up as a victory if they can unhinge or create doubts in the hearts of runners.

So a good test to apply when the devils of dropping-out accost you is this one which I have borrowed from the editors of *The Jogger* (the newsletter of the National Jogging Association): "Take a look at who's giving you the flack, then take a look at yourself. Who looks better? Who seems to have more energy? Who feels better? Who is smoking the cigarette? Who is overweight? Who is hypertense? Who do you think is actually reaping the highest quality of life?"

My point is this: There exists a conscious or unconscious complex among non-runners—a complex against runners, which is compounded of equal parts of guilt and shame about their (the non-runners') sloth. Every time you run by someone who makes a comment about your running, you have evidence of that complex. Beware of the most silver-tongued of these devils; if they can discourage you, they can excuse themselves.

OLD ATHLETES NEVER DIE . . .

Brian marched boldly into my office one day last summer. He stood 6'2", weighed 240 pounds, had a neck the size of my thigh, biceps which were even bigger, and thighs the size of my waist (or so it seemed). He opened with a barrage of braggadocio and hyperbole about his former athletic accomplishments. "I played fullback on my college football team, set a school record in the shot-put, lettered in three sports, etc."

Hardly was this recitation of past glories completed when he launched into his current achievements, "I play a lot of golf and tennis, and recently I've taken up skiing. I can still do a hundred and fifty sit-ups and a hundred push-ups a day. I work out with weights whenever I get the chance." When this discourse was completed I could only ask myself why he was in my office instead of the registration office for the Olympic Decathlon.

Once I ran some tests, I understood. Behind the clearly etched pectorals beat a heart that already showed signs of the man's dissipated, sedentary life-style. His blood pressure was 160/90; his pulse was 92; his cholesterol count 320. He feels out of breath easily and is not sleeping too

Excuses and Their Overcoming

well. He soothes his occasional restlessness and irritability with three or four cocktails before dinner.

When I gave him his jogging prescription, he waxed enthusiastic and assured me that it was "a piece of cake" and "a pleasure." He even offered to race me to the door. He ran with the group for the first week, but won few friends as he ran twice as fast as anyone else and introduced an uncomfortable atmosphere of competition into the proceedings. He would be out of breath near the end of the first mile, but instead of walking ("mere walking," he termed it), he surreptitiously sidled over to his car and went home—well before the group hour was completed. Midway through the second week, Brian was no longer to be seen.

When I called to inquire why he was no longer showing up, he barraged me with the list of exercises and activity he is already engaged in—tennis, golf, weights, etc. Of course, he was exaggerating. Brian exaggerated to preserve his most important possession: his vanity. He simply could not admit to himself or to anyone else, even his doctor, how drastically his fitness had declined since his college days and how much he needed a fitness program.

His excuses were not manufactured to spare him the physical pain of running. As a former athlete, he knows about pain, and may even relish it. Brian feared self-confrontation and psychological pain. His first week of running confirmed his own worst inner fears—he was no longer the person he once was. Rather than continue running—and continuing the climb out of the trough in which he has allowed himself to fall—he preferred to pretend that a few extra holes of golf were all he needed.

I told Brian what I tell other ex-athletes who have fallen from grace and are loath to admit it. Sports, games, and athletics do not by themselves get one in shape. *You have to be in shape before you can play them.* If you are not, you are taking a big risk. Getting into shape means doing aerobic (oxygen-burning) exercise on a regular basis. When you were playing varsity ball in high school or college, it wasn't the weekly game or even the daily practice (with their regular pauses and rests) that kept you in top physical shape. It was the obligatory laps, exercises, diet, and regularity of life-style that maintained your physical condition. When those latter practices diminish or disappear altogether, only a brittle facade remains. Rather than excuse the loss or hide from it, Brian needed to surrender his vanity and begin to rebuild the fitness he had neglected.

GOOD EXCUSES

After all my cold-hearted responses to Herb's "cardiac arrest," Sue's discovery of the danger of running, Brian's vanity, the last thing you expected to see in this chapter was, I am sure, a section on "good" excuses. There are, however, times and conditions that require even the most dedicated of us to forego our running for a day or two. "Good" excuses are based on concrete health or climatic problems of a temporary nature.

Some people, for example, have congenitally weak lungs. They court chills and fever if they run when the temperature dips below 35 degrees. Similarly, if you are suffering from a bad cold, running can become difficult and lead to complications. Waiting for the weather to warm or for your symptoms to dissipate is perfectly acceptable. Friends of mine who live in the San Fernando

Excuses and Their Overcoming

Valley (in Los Angeles) do not run when there is a Stage Two Smog Alert.

The "good" excuse, let me repeat, is one that is temporary and leaves you champing to be out on the running course as soon as possible. The "bad" excuses—the sheer avoiders like "I stayed out too late last night," "my alarm clock did not go off this morning," "relatives are staying with us," etc., ad infinitum—will sooner or later force you to face the one simple question: Do you want to run or don't you? I'm willing to believe that you all have perfectly credible, sound, and reasonable excuses for not running regularly, but I don't want to hear them (nor do I think you really want to hear them either). You can run and be fit or make excuses and be unfit. It is your decision. Should you choose the latter, however, I hope that you have not fooled yourself as to the real reason.

Chapter Eight

RUNNING DIETS

Nine out of ten readers of this book, although they may yearn to regain the lost athletic fitness of their youth, are, secretly, principally interested in running in order to lose weight. The great monkey on the back of American society turns out to be a tire around its middle: flab. No battle is more permanent, more pervasive, more persistently profitless than this one. As the eloquent Dr. George Sheehan has written: "The struggle against the slowly advancing glacier of lard begins before we attain our majority. It never ends. In this war against fat, you have to be a career person."

Sheer willpower is insufficient stuff for this campaign. You may succeed, with great outlays of psychic and physical effort, in shedding five or even ten pounds in an exhilaratingly short period of time, but how permanent will the weight loss be? Unhappily, your and my general experience tell us, not very.

I am not saying that willpower isn't important—my book's message is, I hope, quite the contrary. I am saying that willpower which is not anchored to a *positive* exercise and eating program and set of fitness goals is not enough. Willpower plus running plus nutritional foods is.

Most people come to running in order to lose weight. The bathroom mirror (or the full-length one in your bedroom) is often an even greater enemy than the bathroom scale. Men, for example, distribute their excess weight around a "center of gravity": hips, buttocks, and thighs. An "inch of pinch" in that area usually means about forty pounds of fat, an excess amount for most people since, depending on one's total body weight, the proportion of fat should not exceed 5–10 per cent.

Since most of us carry excess fat, most of us, at one time or another, try to get rid of it. If we can sustain it, fasting is the quickest way to lose weight. I personally cannot sustain it; in fact, I hate the process altogether. Many of those who experience dramatic weight reductions prove incapable of maintenance; slowly, surely, and inexorably their food intake crawls back to the previous level—as does their weight. Food serves a psychological need for them which they have not replaced.

Low-carbohydrate diets also promise quick weight reduction. They produce, however, unwanted side effects. I've been on several of these diets for three or four days at a time and lost five pounds, but I gained severe psychological and physical upsets—e.g., loss of energy, inability to concentrate, irritability, etc. The body needs 60–80 per cent of its food intake to be in the form of carbohydrates, for they are the prime source of the body's energy. When the body is deprived of carbohydrates it begins to operate on protein and fat, thereby producing an acid condition that leads to discomfort. More important, when the body is using protein as energy fuel it is depriving itself of the necessary muscle, cellular, and enzyme building material.

Most "fad diets" not only draw on necessary stores of protein to keep your body functioning, but the weight loss they induce is mostly from loss of water. As soon as you go back to a regular eating program, the water

Running Diets

(hence the pounds) you lost, magically rematerialize around your stomach and hips. These pure dieting programs also produce consistent hunger pains which are psychologically weakening and make almost inhuman demands on our willpower.

The most severe indictment of fad diets, however, is that they are the poorest method of accomplishing our objective: loss of excess fat. My experience with overweight patients has shown me that pure dieting is not only the hardest weight-loss program to adhere to, but that, in comparison with a program combining diet and regular exercise, it pares off less fat and more lean.

In sum, if dieting is to be effective and long lasting, you must feel good about it. But eliminating whole classes of foods entirely from your consumption only invites vitamin deficiencies (hence, low energy and, if continued, poor health) and great psychological discomfort. The way to attack overeating is to undermine the need to overeat, just as the way to stop smoking and reduce alcohol intake is, as we have seen, to become involved in a program whose demands and long-range benefits sap the foundations of the wish to use artificial stimulants.

Weight loss has to occur as a by-product of something positive, something big, something life changing, something that will tie the shedding of pounds into a greater purpose than simple improvement of appearance (as important as that is). There is a role for willpower and a need for self-control, but they are not the heart and soul of my program. Regular running and nutritional foods are. If you follow this latter course, *you can lose weight and keep it off forever*, without a psychologically burdensome load of promises and resolutions. It happens "naturally," through the logic of running.

A running program and your diet are closely related. In fact, these two fitness processes are inseparable, for as soon as you begin to care enough about your body and your health to begin to expend energy to maintain them, you will begin to think twice about the fuel (food) with which you stoke the furnaces.

I want to stress that nutrition (the act of strengthening and promoting one's bodily health through food intake) is not lost when you go on a diet, if the diet is varied and carefully planned. Thus, there is no particular need for you to rush to your local health-food store to stock up on "nutritious" and health-fad foods. If you are overweight, you are overdosed with calories, and many health-store items are similarly overdosed. Carob is a nutritious substitute for chocolate, honey is a nutritious substitute for sugar, and whole wheat bread is far better for you than bread made from white flours containing sucrose, but the caloric content of all these nutritive substitutes is quite high. So keep this in mind—a good vegetable and fruit store is more valuable to you in terms of weight loss and nutrition than a lot of expensive, fattening "health food" items.

While we are on the subject of health-food stores, I want to caution you against the urge to stock up on expensive protein supplements and vitamins. Protein supplements and vitamins have their value for certain people, but they are unnecessary for most. If you exercise a great deal, then increased amounts of vitamin C can be beneficial. Iron is excellent during women's menstrual periods. But excessive amounts of vitamin dosages are equivocal: That is, they certainly do not harm you, but there is no evidence that they help you either. The only sure effect of increased vitamin dosage is increased vita-

Running Diets

min excretion. So if you are interested in having the most expensive perspiration and urine in town, by all means buy as many protein and vitamin supplements as your local health-food store stocks.

Now let's acquaint ourselves with some basic facts. Any time a person expends energy, he burns up calories to fuel the activity. Calories come from food. All activity, even sitting, burns up calories, but naturally there are variations in the number of calories expended in different types of activity (see chart). For example, a typist using an electric machine burns up only 73 calories per hour. A typist using a standard typewriter expends 88 calories per hour, a difference of 15 calories per hour, 90 calories in an average six-hour work day, 450 calories a week. If these two secretaries weigh the same, eat the same amount of food, and metabolize food at the same rate, during a ten-week period, the secretary who uses the standard typewriter will weigh one pound less than the secretary who uses the electric. It's as simple and as inexorable as that. In other words, only a small difference in caloric intake and caloric expenditure during the course of a day, if maintained over a significant period of time, will result in noticeable weight loss and improved body definition.

Knowing (and heeding) all this, how much weight can you expect to lose when you begin to substitute running for typing as your regular form of daily exercise? As a general rule of thumb, if you do not reduce your normal food intake, and if you are not overeating—i.e., actually gaining weight at your current level of caloric ingestion—then the amount of weight you will lose is directly, inexorably related to how much you choose to run. In the beginning, before you're "hooked" on running, you won't be doing more than a mile or two of walking/slogging per day, so your weight loss will be slow: perhaps 1.5 to 2 pounds per month at the most. Here's how.

Jogging is an excellent, probably the best, way of burning up calories; the average jogger burns up approximately 122 calories per mile. A one-mile jog is equivalent, in calorie expenditure, to riding a bike three miles, playing singles tennis for twenty minutes, or swimming for ten straight minutes. Sports, like tennis, and exercises, like swimming and weight lifting, are fine for wind, muscle tone, and the development of the strength and pumping functions of the heart. But calorie burn-up only occurs in the process of playing, stroking, lifting—not during the intermittent rest periods that are endemic to these forms of exercise.

For example, many people feel that if they have spent an hour in the swimming pool, they have burned up some 600 calories (60 × 11.2), whereas, in reality, they have probably only swum for ten or fifteen minutes and burned up only 100 or 150. Similarly, weight lifting will burn up approximately 7–8 calories per minute, but only during the time you are actually huffing and puffing and straining with the weights; simply sitting in the weight room will not rid you of extra calories. Jogging is effective because it is constant, and the rest periods consist of walking, which also burns up about the same amount of calories as a slow jog. The only difference is that the cardiopulmonary benefits of jogging are so much greater than walking.

For every 3,500 calories you ingest, you gain one pound of body weight, so an individual who wishes to lose, say, one pound a week, would have to reduce his or her caloric intake by 500 per day. Actually, two pounds a week is a major accomplishment for most people. This does not mean, of course, that you have to reduce your caloric intake by 1,000 per day. After all, you are a runner now and you are burning up calories on the running track, not to mention toning your muscles and increasing your heart and lung capacity.

A person's metabolic rate will affect his or her ability to lose weight, but not as much or as little as people may think. If you are in good physical condition—that is, you have no thyroid abnormality or other physical or glandular problem—weight reduction will usually be uniform, fluctuating within a predictable range. When I speak of the metabolic rate, I am referring to the measure of energy expended during a resting state of one hour. The average person between the ages of twenty-five and fifty will burn up anywhere from 34–40 calories per hour in this state of non-activity. Males will tend to have a 10–15 per cent higher basal metabolic rate than females due to the male sex hormone, but that does not signify much in terms of one's diet.

Finally, the amount of exertion will determine the percentage increase in metabolism. A short burst of energy can increase one's metabolic rate by as much as 200 per cent; a more sustained, but less powerful burst will increase it 50 per cent. However, it is unlikely that anyone can maintain these extreme strenuous situations for more than a few minutes at a time. The more usual metabolic increase is 25 per cent.

For those of you who are still somewhat unsure of the relationship of your body weight to dieting, etc., I will give you a rule of thumb which should prove useful until you can develop your own sense of proportions. If you want to maintain your weight at a particular level, you multiply that weight by 15, and that will give you the amount of calories you will need to ingest each day. Thus, a 120-pound woman who is satisfied with her weight will need to ingest 1,800 calories a day to maintain it. If she thinks that she would look and feel better at, say, 110 pounds, she must then reduce her calorie intake by 150 (to 1,650). If she cuts out the danish pastry from her coffee break and runs or jogs three miles a day, she will have a 500-calorie deficit daily. At the end of one week she will have lost one pound; ten weeks later she will be at the desired weight.

The point is, she doesn't need to go on any elaborate diet or invoke the fickle, inattentive gods of willpower. Simply by jogging or walking three miles a day—to which, after the first few weeks, she'll become "addicted" anyway (hence, requiring willpower to stop)—she will be making a major contribution to weight loss. In addition to this, if she utilizes her willpower for the very modest task of cutting out a dessert or two, she will have solved her problem in several months . . . and the problem won't return.

At this point it will be useful for you to examine the Calorie Expenditure Chart. If you are aware of the number of calories you use up in each activity in which you engage, then you will be more aware of how many calories you are allowed to ingest during the day. Familiarity with the chart will also enhance your ability to regulate your daily diet. I absolutely implore the readers of this book to be cognizant of the calories going in and out of their bodies.

By knowing the caloric expenditure of miles jogged, and keeping in mind your caloric intake of food, you can calculate the rate at which you will lose poundage. Don't

Running Diets

rush yourself and don't make unrealistic demands on your willpower. In your anxiety to lose weight, don't accelerate your daily amounts of jogging beyond a reasonable and enjoyable number of miles. *Trust to the process of the running;* it has a logic of its own. It will invade your psyche in its own good time, and you will only obstruct

CALORIE EXPENDITURE CHART

COMPARATIVE CALORIC EXPENDITURE PER MINUTE

Walking 2 mph	2.8	Resting in bed	1.2
Walking 3.5 mph	4.8	Sitting	1.4
Bicycling 5.5 mph	3.2	Sitting and eating	1.6
Bicycling rapidly	6.9	Playing cards	1.7
Running 5.7 mph	12.0	Standing	1.6
Running 7 mph	14.5	Kneeling	1.4
Swimming 2.2 mph	26.7	Squatting	2.2
Golf	5.0	Showering	3.7
Tennis	7.1		
Table tennis	5.8	Walking upstairs	20.0
Dancing	5.2	Walking downstairs	7.6
Billiards	3.0		
Sailing	2.6	Machine sewing	1.5
Bowling	8.1	Sweeping	1.7
Badminton	2.8	Washing clothes	2.9
		Peeling vegetables	2.9
		Stirring and mixing	3.0
		Ironing	4.2
		Making beds	5.3

Carrying tools	3.6
Chopping wood	4.9
Sawing wood	6.9

COMPARATIVE CALORIC EXPENDITURE PER HOUR (PARTICULAR)

Walking slowly	200	Sleeping	65
Carpentry	240	Lying still	77
Swimming	500	Sitting	100
Running	570	Standing	105

COMPARATIVE CALORIC EXPENDITURE PER HOUR (GENERAL)

Sedentary activities (reading, watching television, writing, eating, sewing)	10–40
Light activities (cooking, ironing, or any activity that involves standing with some arm movement)	50–100
Moderate activities (light housework, light gardening, carpentry)	110–180
Vigorous activities (heavy housework, bowling, dancing, horseback riding, skating, calisthenics)	190–270
Strenuous activities (manual labor, fast cycling, swimming, climbing, running, tennis, skiing, vigorous sexuality)	300–700

and decelerate this process if you get too hung up about weight loss.

In the beginning, especially, don't set hard and fast standards for what your optimal body weight should be. When you feel comfortable with the look, feel, and tone of your body—and when these things, plus your weight, are a *natural expression of your new, running self*—then you have achieved your optimal body weight. So forget the charts and forget about making long-range plans of what you now think you want to weigh. It will happen naturally with the running process. No need for premature second guessing.

Despite all I have said about trusting to the running process and accepting weight loss as a natural by-product of larger physical and mental changes, I realize there will still be anxious readers who want accelerated and predictable schedules of losing weight. For those of you who are really in desperate earnest about shedding pounds, my main advice would be to increase the number of miles you cover each day, *but not by an unrealistic number*. If you're just starting out, then try walking two miles instead of one. Don't run or even jog, by the way, because if you're badly overweight, you'll only strain yourself needlessly at the outset. What you might want to start doing is this: Walk or (if you're beyond the first week or two of your program) jog your usual amount of distance, and *then add one (at most, two) more mile* for the sake of losing flab. You can call them "flab miles" if you like, but don't go beyond this or you'll risk derailing your commitment to the entire running program.

Let me also repeat: For the sake of your commitment to the larger program and its goals and process, try hard not to fret overly about your weight. Fretting gets in the way of positive mental energy, and we'll need that energy for greater goals than mere weight loss. Concentrate on other things—the nutritive value of your food, your running, ways of deriving increased meaning from your running time (whether with people or alone), etc. Above all, don't be excessively harsh on yourself about exclusionary diets—i.e., cutting yourself off wholesale from most of the foods you love. This will block the positive frame of mind we need.

There are some specific things for you, the weight-obsessed beginning runner, to do. For one thing, don't weigh yourself too often—it'll only increase your compulsion. And for another, be patient, especially in the beginning when weight loss will be primarily loss of water due to perspiration in your running. This is deceptive because you'll replace the weight as soon as you take a drink of water or iced tea, and this will discourage you if you've allowed false expectations to arise.

Next, let's finally talk about willpower and take advantage of your good, strong will which is probably flooding over you right now as you make plans to get going in a running program. You probably have between twenty-four and seventy-two hours of really strong will in you, so let's get ourselves off to a bang of a start—not because you'll lose a whole lot of poundage (though you may dump two or three permanently) but because a good start is important for the long haul. For the first day at least, a certain sense of sacrifice and masochism can be useful, particularly since so many readers will be bent on "proving" themselves anyway.

If you wish, then, try a twenty-four hour fast. Avoid solid foods and drink as much liquid as necessary (water, coffee, tea, sugar-free soft drinks, fruit juice) to still the rumblings in your stomach. You may, as a result, have provided yourself with the necessary stimulus for a dieting regime. (I do, however, want to caution you against excessive intake of coffee and tea while dieting. More than three cups of coffee or tea a day can cause gastric acidity, stomach upset, and, perhaps, ulcers. Remember also that one cup of coffee contains 90 milligrams of caffein, one cup of tea contains 50, one cup of Sanka 18, and one diet soda 30. Excess caffein can cause heart palpitations, insomnia, irritability, and anxiety. As in all aspects of your running and your diet, do not overdo a good thing.)

Running Diets

Once past this introductory phase, however (and don't fast for more than one day or it will interrupt your running program) the going gets a bit tougher: snacks must be minimized *but not eliminated.* A snack is an essential part of dieting (indeed, many people think it is an essential part of life), but you must change the content of the snack. Ice cream, candy, pie, cake, pretzel, Frito, or potato-chip snacks are out; carrot and celery sticks, pickles (dill, unsweetened, kosher), and apples are in.

In terms of the actual diet itself, the changes in what you eat should be gradual and occur over a significant amount of time. The willpower you have will be needed for your jogging program, and you should not overextend yourself at first by adding on an overconcern with food decrease and weight reduction. It is best if you concentrate on building toward the addictive stage of jogging before embarking on the possibly traumatic scenario of a crash diet.

I generally suggest that people who want to lose weight by running and dieting should cut their caloric intake by 500 per day. But not the first day! That is far too big a morsel to digest. You should begin with 100 or 200 calories a day, slowly working your way toward the 500 level. The changes in eating must be as gradual as the increases in running minutes; otherwise you will encourage discouragement.

I have provided three separate weight-loss diets that stress nutritive foods. One is geared to a 1,000 calorie daily in-take, one to 1,500, and the third to 2,000. Depending on your metabolic rate (i.e., the number of calories you burn up in a normal day), depending on how much you are walking/jogging, and depending on how fast you wish to lose weight, you may pick one of these three around which to orient your eating for the next month or two. But there is no need to be slavish because, remember, the important thing is your getting hooked on the running program and deriving the larger benefits accruing from it.

If you select the 1,500-calorie diet, and if you're burning up between 300–500 calories in your jogging, then you should start to lose weight at the rate of 2–3 pounds per week. Much more than that would not be healthy, and there would be no need for a swifter rate of loss. If you decide to eat a bit more in the course of any given day, then remember to add the extra "flab mile" on your running. If for some *very good, very unusual* reason (which should NOT occur often), you miss your daily jogging, then cut your food intake by 300–500 calories.

Any diet is impossible to maintain if you keep high-calorie foods around the house. Plan ahead for those special days and holidays when you know you will be tanking up on calories. Increase your jogging slightly and decrease your eating the next day. The main thing always is the running. Even if you're not strong-willed enough to cut back much on your eating, your running will slowly take off its measure of weight.

In the meantime, though, keep well informed of the exact number of calories you are putting into your stomach. Try to construct an internal "foodometer" in your mind which compulsively counts calories and rings a buzzer when the magic number of 1,500 is reached. Add all calories from snacks as well as meals to the foodometer, but remember to subtract the calories expended at jogging and exercises (if you do five minutes of stretchies, that's 35 calories right there).

1,000 CALORIE DIET

		Quantity	Calories
BREAKFAST:	Dry cereal	2 cups	200
	Vegetable juice	1 glass	25
	Skim milk	1 cup	80
	Coffee or tea	1 cup	0
	Total		305
LUNCH:	One head of lettuce		40
	Diet dressing	4 tbs.	100
	Apple	1	100
	Carrot	1	25
	Cauliflower	1 cup	20
	Total		285
DINNER:	One head of lettuce		40
	Diet dressing	4 tbs.	100
	Apples (one of which should be eaten before dinner to take the edge off your appetite)	2	200
	Cauliflower	2 cups	40
	Shrimp, crab meat, lobster, filet of sole or flounder, or two slices of cheese	1 cup	200–250
	Total		580–630
	Total Complete		1,170–1,220
SNACKS:	Coffee, tea, diet soda, cauliflower, carrots, celery, or lettuce		

2,000 CALORIE DIET

		Quantity	Calories
BREAKFAST:	Apple, orange, or half cantaloupe	1	100
	Orange juice	½ cup	50
	Cereal, dry	1 cup	100
	Toast	2 slices	150
	Butter	2 pats	100
	Beverage (Sanka, tea, bouillon)	1 cup	0
	Total		500
LUNCH:	Apple, orange, or half cantaloupe	1	100
	Salad, large	1	200
	Dressing	2 tbs.	200
	Beverage	1 cup	0
	Total		500
DINNER:	Apple, orange, or half cantaloupe	1	100
	Salad, large	1	200
	Dressing	2 tbs.	200
	Cooked vegetables	1 cup	300
	Beverage	1 cup	0
	Fish or poultry	1 cup	200
	Total		1,000
	Total Complete		2,000

Use calorie chart above along with exchange chart excluding meat products.

3,000 CALORIE DIET

		Quantity	Calories
BREAKFAST:	Apple, orange, or half cantaloupe	1	100
	Orange or apple juice	1 cup	100
	Cereal, dry or cooked	2 cups	200
	Toast	2 slices	150
	Butter	2 pats	100
	Beverage (Sanka, tea, bouillon)	2 cups	0
	Total		650
LUNCH:	Apple, orange, or half cantaloupe	1	100
	Salad, large	1	200
	Dressing	2 tbs.	200
	Beverage	1 cup	0
	Dessert	1	200
	Total		700
DINNER:	Apple, orange, or half cantaloupe	1	100
	Salad, extra large	1	250
	Dressing	3 tbs.	300
	Beverage	1 cup	0
	Cooked vegetables	2 cups	600
	Fish or poultry	2 cups	400
	Total		1,650
	Total Complete		3,000

Use calorie chart above along with exchange chart excluding meat products.

EXCHANGE CHART

*Basic Rules to Follow
For Dr. Mollen's
1,000, 2,000, and 3,000
Calorie Semi-veggy Diets*

1. No red meats, veal, or pork
2. No refined sugars
3. No peanut butter, jam, candy, cookies, or mints
4. No milk, other than in coffee
5. No salt
6. Avoidance of breads—once weekly
7. Chicken once or twice monthly
8. Fish every other day, if desired
9. Lettuce, one head daily at least
Salad dressing: lemon, oil (2 tablespoons at most) and vinegar and one package of Sweet 'n Low
10. Apples—three daily at least (one at breakfast, lunch, and dinner)
11. Vegetables—raw or boiled, no butter, at least every other day
12. Two tablespoons of bran daily with breakfast
13. Granola cereal with no preservatives (preferably dry—no milk)
14. Most fruits except pineapple, watermelon, honeydew, grapes
15. Baked potatoes—no butter or sour cream
16. Eggs—once or twice weekly if desired
17. Nuts are allowed but are high in calories—1,000 cal. = 1 cup
18. Be aware of caloric content of every food you eat
19. Diet sodas help to suppress appetite
20. Between-meal snacks—use bouillon, coffee, tea, diet sodas, or raw vegetables
21. No foods with preservatives

Running Diets

To help your foodometer, especially at the outset of your diet, write down the foods you tend to eat, starring those that have an especially large caloric content. Each day, write down the food and the calories you have ingested at *every* meal and *every* snack. You should be able to tell anyone who asks, at any time of the day, how many calories you have consumed up to that point. Once you become aware of the "numbers game," the rest becomes a lot easier.

All of these aids and signposts—the calorie chart, the foodometer, the "numbers game"—will lead nowhere, however, if they are not securely anchored in a regular running program. Running, by changing your perspective on your life and your self, provides the incentive to improve your eating habits and maintain your new shape and condition. Willpower is a necessary adjunct to continued running and decreased caloric intake, but it too is out of shape. Your willpower needs the conditioning of a regular running program as much as your muscles, lungs, heart, and waistline do.

Chapter Nine

A RUNNING SEMINAR WITH DR. MOLLEN

A RUNNING SEMINAR WITH DOCTOR MOLLEN

Q: Is there an age limit?
A: My five-year-old son jogs, and I have an eighty-year-old patient who jogs. There is no real age limit for the young, provided they are not forced into it, or for the elderly, provided they undergo a proper medical evaluation and have been given an exercise prescription to fit their capacity.

Brad, my son, started jogging along with me at the tail end of my run. He would wait for me at the beginning of the last half mile of my run. In the beginning he could hardly jog half of that continuously. After three weeks, he was running two miles.

If the child can walk adequately and is not pushed into it by his parents, no age is too young.

In Los Angeles, recently, a five-year-old ran thirty miles in five hours. He was entered in a twenty-six-mile marathon, got lost along the way, ran four extra miles, and still almost broke his age-group record.

Q: How much exercise should I begin with?
A: A mile. Walk it, jog it, crawl it, beg, borrow, or steal it, but cover that single mile every day. Do this distance

every day for thirty days, and you will have consumed the minimal addictive dose.

Q: How much should I increase, and how fast should I increase past the original mile?

A: In general, I recommend an increase of one mile every four weeks.

Q: Is it better to run a longer distance slower or a shorter distance faster?

A: I would prefer to see you run three miles at a slower speed as opposed to running one mile as fast as you can. With a longer distance you are not only burning more calories, but are sustaining your cardiovascular exertion at an elevated level for a prolonged period of time. Longer distances also enable you to enjoy the mental aspects of jogging and lessen the discomfort and strain.

Q: How should I breathe?

A: Normally. As long as your breathing is relaxed, the manner is unimportant.

Q: Will I lose more weight if I sweat more?

A: You will lose your weight in water, but that is only temporary. Two glasses of water will put those pounds right back on. The object is to exercise, not to sweat.

Q: What is the effect of air pollution on my lungs?

A: You will be in better health if you jog in a polluted area than by not jogging in a clear-air environment. Studies are now in progress to determine the exact relationship of jogging to inhalation of pollution, but those that have been completed indicate that a jogger inhales less pollution than someone out walking. The jogger, with his or her tremendously developed cardiovascular system has a 25 per cent absorption rate

A Running Seminar with Dr. Mollen

compared to a walker, who might absorb 95 per cent. In any event, morning runners inhale less pollution than evening runners, so that is another incentive to get out there early—you beat the exhaust brigade.

Q: Should I jog in cold weather?

A: Yes, but dress warmly. Gloves and a cap are strongly recommended when the mercury drops below forty. When the thermometer dips into the teens, breathing becomes difficult. You should wear a filter-type surgical mask, which serves to warm the air before it goes into your respiratory system. Dr. Terrance Cavanaugh of Toronto, Canada, has many cardiac patients who jog in very cold weather. He has designed an apparatus for them that consists of a tube (placed under one's sweatshirt) attached to a surgical mask. The heat of the body thus warms the air.

Q: What about hot weather?

A: If the temperature exceeds ninety degrees, you are courting heat-stroke syndrome unless you take precautions. For every three miles you intend to jog, take in at least 16 ounces of fluid to compensate for the dehydration. Wear minimal clothing that fits very loosely to allow for proper evaporation of perspiration. If you wear a top, make it a nylon mesh one. Wear a hat if you are jogging at midday. The symptoms of heat-stroke syndrome are nausea, dizziness, abdominal cramps, severe fatigue, and, if really serious, dry and clammy skin. If you experience any of these symptoms while running, get to a cool place as soon as possible and drink sufficient fluid to replace the liquid you have lost. Do not fool with this malady: it can be quite serious and it can precipitate other problems.

Q: Should I run at night?
A: Potentially, it is quite dangerous. If you run in a park, you will not be able to see uneven ground or holes. If you run in the street, cars will not be able to see you. But if you must, wear white clothes and attach reflectors or reflector tape to your running clothes. Run facing traffic.

Q: Should I wear a sweat suit while jogging?
A: It is not necessary. Your legs warm up very quickly during a run and thus need little protection from the cold. When the mercury drops below forty degrees, a sweat shirt reduces the amount of heat loss from the body and protects against wind chill.

In warm weather, a sweat suit is harmful. Sweating is not the name of this game. When you sweat you lose important minerals and electrolytes, precisely the elements your body needs to protect against heat-stroke syndrome.

Q: What other accessories do you consider good to carry or wear while running?
A: If you tend to sweat excessively, I would recommend a head band. It absorbs a great deal of water and keeps the salty perspiration from running into and stinging your eyes.

Men should wear a good athletic supporter.

Women should wear bras.

Low-cut socks are sometimes better because they have less of a tendency to slip down into the shoe and become bunched up there.

If your nose tends to run, by all means carry a handkerchief or some tissue in your running shorts. Blowing in the wind is not satisfying—and it is somewhat primitive.

A Running Seminar with Dr. Mollen

If your thighs tend to get chafed during a run, spread some petroleum jelly on before starting or carry a small tube with you.

Q: Should I eat or drink before running?

A: I recommend running on nothing more than a glass of water. Eating can give you a full or bloated feeling which makes running uncomfortable; eating or drinking can precipitate bowel movements or urination in the middle of the run. Other runners, like Frank Shorter, prefer not to run on an empty stomach and may eat a banana, a piece of cheese, or a teaspoon or two of peanut butter before they start out. It is all a matter of personal preference, but try to avoid running directly after banquets.

Q: Should women run?

A: Of course. Absolutely. Immediately.

Q: How far and how fast?

A: As far and as fast as it feels comfortable. There is little difference in the progression rates for men and women.

Q: During the menstrual period, can a woman continue to run?

A: There are no studies which indicate any harm occuring to women who run during the time of their period. On the other hand, women have set records during the Olympics while menstruating. If you are severely cramped, running will be difficult. The best advice I can give you is to become knowledgeable about your body and its limits, then act accordingly. I must point out, however, that running is one of the best ways I know to discover your body and its limits.

Q: During pregnancy?

A: Doctors believe that pregnant women should carry on

with their accustomed activities as long as they are comfortable. This includes jogging. Avoid wind sprints, interval training, or steep hills, because they cut down the amount of oxygen going to the fetus. Otherwise, a study by a Hungarian doctor showed that the duration of labor was shorter for active than non-active females.

Q: Is there a particularly good shoe for women?

A: There are several shoes that run narrower and generally fit a woman's foot more adequately. There are shoes that are lighter weight and more flexible which some women prefer, especially if they are petite. I recommend for women the Nike Waffle Trainer, Nicki Cortez, the Adidas SL70, and the Puma 9190. Petite women should try to stay away from shoes that have excessively thick soles. Yet heavier women might want to go to a shoe that does have a heavier sole.

Q: Can a woman train to run a marathon just as men do?

A: Absolutely yes. Many women in this country have run marathons quite successfully with times that some men wish they could break (including myself). Actually, women are more suited to run ultra-marathons (distances of 50 miles and more) due to their increased percentage of body fat. A woman has approximately 25 per cent body fat as opposed to a man who has approximately 15 per cent. Increased amount of body fat represents increased amount of energy at longer distances. One gram of fat equals 9 calories of energy.

Q: What's the best way to deal with a "stitch" while running?

A: Most runners can resolve the stitch if they lean forward while running and put pressure on the area; or by slowing their pace and not allowing as much stretching of the diaphragm. If you are constantly bothered by stitches, change your dietary habits, reducing milk intake and decreasing the amount of acid foods (orange juices, cantaloupes, etc.).

Q: How should I treat my blisters?

A: With care. Do not run on an unprotected popped or open blister. Cover it with gauze, moleskin, and tape. Tender areas can be covered with petroleum jelly to protect them during the run. Pay special attention to the fit of your socks and shoes. If you run without socks, talcum or athlete's or baby powder on the inside of the shoes will alleviate the friction and heat.

Q: Do orthotics help running injuries?

A: Orthotics are plastic inserts placed in the shoes. If a runner is having a problem with his feet, ankles, knees, or even hips, these plastic inserts sometimes allow the foot to strike the ground in a more biomechanically correct manner. Biomechanic disorders will not appear while walking because the foot does not strike the ground as often or as hard.

Orthotics, however, are not the ultimate cure of all runners' injuries. Before inserting them into your shoe, you should experiment with the five S's: stretching, style, shoes, speed, surface. Stretching is the best preventative and the best cure of runners' injuries.

Q: I have low-back pain, can I still run?

A: Running will probably benefit you greatly. Most low-back pain is caused by tension which leads to muscle spasms. Running relaxes one immensely, and should help lessen the pains—unless the source of your pain is a disc injury. In any event, you should see your physician for an X ray and a diagnosis.

Q: Can long-term jogging cause arthritis?

A: There is no medical evidence to indicate that jogging alters arthritic conditions one way or the other. In and of itself, jogging will not cause arthritic knees. In fact, jogging promotes circulation in the knee area and decreases the amount of calcium deposits that might otherwise form there.

Runners who have knee problems generally have a constitutional weakness there to begin with, or have injured it or weakened it in some other activity, or have run for a long time on very hard surfaces.

Q: I have heard that some people have had heart attacks while jogging. What about that?

A: Those people have gone out and jogged too fast, too soon. They have neglected a medical evaluation and proper supervision. Everyone over thirty-five should have a stress-EKG before beginning a running program.

Q: Is there a special diet for joggers?

A: No. I recommend an increase in the consumption of fruits and vegetables and a decrease in the amounts of red meat, milk, butter, and eggs. My diet consists of 70 per cent carbohydrates, 20 per cent proteins, and 10 per cent fats.

Q: Should I drink milk as part of my new diet?

A: No. For one thing, milk is very high in cholesterol. For another, after the first decade of one's life, milk is no longer the staff of life. In fact, for many it is harmful. Ten per cent of all Caucasians, for example, are allergic to it. The other 90 per cent no longer have the digestive enzyme capacity to handle the milk as thoroughly as when they were children, thus they may experience diarrhea, cramps, or abdominal bloating if they run after imbibing "nature's most perfect food."

Q: Is cheese a good snack?

A: Yes, but in small amounts, meaning no more than two ounces a day. Cheese is both high in calories (100 calories per ounce) and cholesterol. Thus, you pay a high price for getting your protein in this form.

Q: And yogurt?

A: It too is high in cholesterol and calories and, in my opinion, possesses no other essential ingredients than other, similar foods.

Q: Should I take vitamins now that I am running?

A: Believe it or not, if you eat well-balanced, nutritional meals, you will be getting all the vitamins you need. If you are under an excessive amount of stress, however, I would recommend an increased amount of vitamin C, not to exceed 1,000 mg. daily. Iron supplements are sometimes helpful. The recommended daily allowance for males is 10 mg.; for females, 18. Increased intake of other vitamins will be lost through perspiration or urination.

Q: What about protein supplements?

A: You get adequate protein from cereals, bread, rice, potatoes, fish, chicken, and, of course, red meat. In fact, the body can go thirty days without protein and not suffer any devastating effects. Excess protein, on the other hand, has a tendency to leave you lethargic and fatigued.

Q: Why do you advise against red meat?

A: Red meat contains excessive amounts of calories and cholesterol and is not digested as well or as fast as vegetables.

Q: How many calories are burned off through jogging?
A: You burn up between 100 and 122 calories every mile you jog, no matter what speed you are running.
Q: How many pounds a week can I expect to lose?
A: Two pounds.
Q: Will hill running improve my lung capacity?
A: Yes, but unless you are training for the 1980 Olympics avoid hills until you are an advanced runner. For the beginning and intermediate runner, hills cause more soreness and injuries than benefits.
Q: How long should I have been running before I attempt my first marathon?
A: It varies, but generally between three and nine months.
Q: How much running should I do to prepare for a marathon?
A: You should run at least 30 miles a week for 10 weeks prior to the marathon. To run it comfortably (especially the last 6 miles) I would recommend 60–80 miles a week.

You should begin preparing at least three months in advance. The first month's goal should be 6 miles a day; the second month, 10 miles a day. For the third month—just prior to the marathon—I would advise two-hour runs on alternate days, with light stretching and jogging in between.

Training schedule for a half marathon:

first week	*second week*	*third week*
S 5 miles	S 5 miles	S 5 miles
M 3 miles	M 4 miles	M 5 miles
T 4 miles	T 4 miles	T 3 miles
W 8 miles	W 8 miles	W 10 miles

T 3 miles   T 3 miles   T 3 miles
F 4 miles   F 6 miles   F 8 miles
S 5 miles   S 6 miles   S 6 miles

fourth week

S 10 miles
M light
T 10 miles
W light
T 10 miles
F light
S light
Marathon

Drink as much fluid as you need during a marathon. Water is the best fluid; juices and Gatorade may upset your stomach.

Q: Should I drink fluids during a marathon or half-marathon?

A: Absolutely, water is the best, though some runners find that Gatorade or orange slices help. However, these and other fluids may upset your stomach while running, try them before you take them in the race.

Q: What is carbohydrate loading?

A: Eating excessive amounts of starches three days prior to the marathon. You should stay within the normal calorie intake range of your diet, but feast only on bread, potatoes, pancakes, pasta, etc.

Q: What does carbohydrate loading do?

A: It allows your body to store more glycogen. This glycogen is a handy reserve twenty miles into the marathon, when your normal amount of energy begins to run out. It is then converted to glucose and sent into the blood stream thereby obtaining an elevated blood-sugar level and increased energy.

Q: I just want to keep fit—you can keep your marathons. How much running should I do?

A: Thirty minutes a day (3–3.5 miles), five days a week. Five physical fitness experts with whom I talked prior to the last Boston Marathon agreed that this program would promote peak physical fitness in the average person.

Q: What does "aerobic" mean?

A: The constant exchange of oxygen with the environment. In aerobic exercise there is an increased exchange of oxygen and carbon dioxide between you and the environment. As a result, your cardiovascular system is stressed to the point where its capacity increases. Aerobic activities are those that require a heightened and sustained level of interchange: jogging, walking, swimming, bicycling, rowing, handball, racquetball, squash. In general, however, activities with rest periods built in are not good, i.e., tennis, golf.

Q: What about days off?

A: Never take more than one or two days off weekly. The benefits you derive from running—both physical and mental—stem from the constancy and repetition of the exercise: habituation.

Q: Are there any magazines devoted to running?

A: *Runner's World*, P.O. Box 366, Mt. View, California 94040.

National Jogging Association, 1910 K Street N.W., Washington, D.C. 20006.

A.M.J.A. Newsletter, P.O. Box 4704, North Hollywood, California 91607.

Chapter Ten

STAYING WITH IT

The message of this book has never been that running is easy, but rather that getting hooked on running isn't hard. Ten minutes a day—approximately one mile—is all it takes. It is not enough by itself to give you total fitness, but it is enough to break you out of the bind of your current inertia, to give you a foretaste of the physical and psychological benefits of running, and to make your body and mind crave larger doses. Ten minutes a day for twelve weeks, therefore, won't by itself be nirvana, but it will put you on the running track that leads there.

One of the nice things about this heaven-on-earth is that it regularly returns to you more than you invest. The activity of running makes total demands on your body, to be sure—your oxygen-burning system, your blood-transport system, your skeletal frame, your muscles, your nervous system, and your co-ordination. Very little, including your mind and spirit, escapes a workout from the demands made by LSD running. The great paradox of this exercise is that the great demands made in a regular way by daily running are paid back a hundredfold in increased efficiency, stamina, strength. Running may take your all, but it gives back your all with compound interest: better frame of mind, improved muscle tone, greater flexibility, and, above all, heightened endurance. Running makes you endure.

This notion of endurance is the key to what running does for your life and your consciousness. More than any activity I know, running forces you to concentrate on the moment, to *feel* the present—almost to the point of stopping time and holding on to it. Long Slow Distance running makes time slow way down. It brings the runner face to face with the now. In certain moments, as we saw in Chapter Four, the sense of time may even disappear altogether, and you will arrive at the end of your run with little recall of the minutes spent arriving there.

The slowing down of the time spectrum is critically important in our age of deadlines, appointments, plans, ambitions, drives, intentions, schedules. The source of much of our stress lies in our chronic inability to fit everything into what we have come to experience as too short a day; and the harder we try to do it all, the less we seem able to do anything. Running revalues that fundamental currency called time—the only currency that finally matters in our lives; the currency we spend frivolously and wantonly and unknowingly. Running fills each minute with sixty seconds lived. Running is a cornucopia spilling over with effort, with thought, with feeling, with heightened sensations, with visions, with co-ordination, and with joy. There is, on occasion, pain also; but pain, too, can be good and instructive. Running fills you with momentary freedom from all drives because the drive to run needs all your effort. There are times, even, when running "fills" you with simple regenerative void.

This may sound unbelievable to the person who has not run—it may sound like the false promises of the street corner evangelizer. To the doubters I would only say this:

Ask anyone—*anyone*—who runs, how they feel about running, about themselves, about life, and they will tell you that from wherever they were before they took up daily running, they now feel a whole lot better. I've never known anyone who in all honesty would contend otherwise. I have known many people who started running and stopped, but they will always admit that while they ran, they felt better . . . and most of them will come back to running, or intend to do so, as their lives once again fill up with stress and unhappiness. People who have run and then have stopped probably never knew the LSD running we've talked about in this book. These people probably ran for speed, trophies, records, or against some internal clock or set of demands and expectations. They never gave real running a chance. They probably stopped because they got busy with other things, and they had no addiction to running to see them through such temptations to quit. For them the daily or weekly bout with the clock was simply one more contest in a life filled with competition, demands, striving.

Some people who do know the value of LSD running, who have been hooked on it, may stop for a spell. Perhaps they are on the move—traveling and away from the familiar environment that made running easy—or their lives are momentarily filled up with too many diversions and demands. They will always come back as gradually their bodies and minds suffer from running's absence.

I know there will be some hard-core skeptics out in the world who will never run for a variety of reasons and excuses. They probably won't be reading this book, and even if they do, there is nothing more I could say to convince them of my message. The readers who are heavily on my mind just now, however, are the people who, though essentially in agreement with me that their lives would be uplifted and the bodies mended from daily jogging along LSD lines, simply won't do it because they won't get around to starting. These are the people who can't be moved by good advice and rousing rhetoric, and even their own wishes and intentions won't suffice to actually get them started.

I have a close friend who used to be a patient. I got him started on LSD running four years ago. He is a highly intellectual young man who used to lead a sedentary life-style. It was not really hard to get him running; he was addicted within a few months, and he continues to run now. One day as we jogged together, I could sense a heaviness in Ed's heart. I asked him about it. It seems that a close relative of his—a beloved uncle—had died an untimely death from a coronary at age forty-seven. "Dale was more than an uncle to me," Ed said. "He was really a father, for I never knew my real father. When I was a kid, Dale taught me many sports—swimming, hunting, water-skiing. He was the symbol of health, fitness, and vitality to me. When I grew up and moved away from home and his influence, Dale always did the best he could to see that I kept up some marginal interest in sports. Thanks to him I played tennis and skied; and mostly thanks to him I never felt comfortable with myself and my life during the years I put on weight and lost the fitness of my youth. More than anything else, it was my uncle's voice, deep within my unconscious, that made me so open and accessible to your message four years ago, Art. I ran *with* you because you were my doctor and my friend, but I ran *for* my uncle Dale, to show him that I had never totally forgotten the values of body and mind he had instilled in me when I was young."

APPENDIX A

DR. MOLLEN'S GUIDELINES TO EASY JOGGING

1) *Age and Sex:* Doesn't matter, advance to successive levels at your own pace with consideration as to what you are comfortable with.

2) *Warm-up:* Stretching exercises—5 minutes. All levels.

3) *Cool down:* Five minutes of walking—all levels.

4) *Time:* Essentially unimportant.

5) Never jog at a speed at which you cannot carry on a normal conversation.

6) *Style:* Heel-to-toe motion.

7) *Footwear:* Proper jogging shoes only.

8) *Surface:* (1) Dirt—best, (2) Grass, (3) Asphalt, (4) Concrete—worst.

Level 1	Beginners
Distance	1 mile
Style	Walk-jog
Days/Wk.	7
Time	Unimportant—just cover the distance

Level 2	Intermediate Beginners
Distance	2 miles
Style	Walk-jog
Days/Wk.	7
Time	Unimportant
Level 3	Advanced Beginners
Distance	3 miles
Style	Walk-jog
Days/Wk.	7
Time	Unimportant
Level 4	Intermediate #1
Distance	3 miles
Style	Walk-jog
Days/Wk.	6–7
Time	30–33 minutes
Level 5	Intermediate #2
Distance	4 miles
Style	Walk-jog
Days/Wk.	6–7
Time	40–44 minutes
Level 6	Intermediate #3
Distance	5 miles
Style	Walk-jog
Days/Wk.	6–7
Time	50–55 minutes

P.H.E.—Degree Granted (Pump-Heart-Efficiently)

Levels beyond this are optional—total physical fitness has been obtained at this level.

Appendix

Level 7　　　　　　Advanced #1

Distance　　　　　6 miles
Style　　　　　　　Jog
Days/Wk.　　　　　6–7
Time　　　　　　　60 minutes

Level 8　　　　　　Advanced #2

Distance　　　　　6–8 miles
Style　　　　　　　Jog
Days/Wk.　　　　　6–7
Time　　　　　　　60–80 minutes

Level 9　　　　　　Advanced #3

Distance　　　　　8–10 miles
Style　　　　　　　Jog
Days/Wk.　　　　　6–7
Time　　　　　　　80–100 minutes

Level 10　　　　　Attempt a Marathon—26 miles 385 yards

Distance　　　　　10 miles
Style　　　　　　　Jog
Days/Wk.　　　　　6–7
Time　　　　　　　90–100 minutes

APPENDIX B

DR. MOLLEN'S SURVEY OF THE AMERICAN MEDICAL JOGGER'S ASSOCIATION

300 Physicians Surveyed
Age Range: 25–60

1. How many miles do you run weekly?
   - 25 or more 60%
   - 50 or more 30%
   - 60 or more 10%
   - 70 or more 0%
2. How many marathons have you run?
   Range: 0–85, #14—1st marathon
3. Have you ever had a running injury over the past year?
   - Yes 60%
   - No 40%
4. Where is your most common injury sustained?
   - Achilles 15%
   - Foot 10%
   - Ankle 15%
   - Leg 10%
   - Knee 38%
   - Hip 5%
   - Back 5%
   - Groin 1%

Appendix

5. Do you wear orthotics?
   Yes 20%
   No 80%
6. Has your injury been totally resolved?
   Yes 40%
   No 60%
7. How important do you value stretching exercises?
   Very 50%
   Moderate 35%
   Minimally 15%
8. Do you train by the LSD (Long Slow Distance) method?
   Yes 70%
   Interval training 30%
9. Do you think beer has a significant value in marathon running?
   Yes 35%
   No 65%
10. Do you eat any red meats at all?
    Yes 80%
    No 20%
11. Do you ingest any vitamin C supplementation daily?
    Yes 75%
    No 25%
12. Which shoe do you run in the most? Check one.
    Nike 40%
    Adidas 20%
    Brooks 10%
    New Balance 15%
    Pony 10%
    Tiger ___
    Etonic ___
    Puma 5%
    Other ___

13. Which of the following do you feel most effective in the control of heart disease? Check one.
    Diet alone ___
    Exercise alone 20%
    Diet and exercise 80%
14. Do you feel a low cholesterol diet maintaining you at 150 mg. of cholesterol or less will give you moderate cardiovascular immunization without exercise?
    Yes 30%
    No 70%
15. Do you feel daily exercise of 60 minutes of jogging will give you cardiovascular immunization?
    Yes 80%
    No 20%
16. What do you drink during a marathon? Check one.
    Water 70%
    Gatorade 10%
    ERG 9%
    Nothing 1%
    Beer 5%
    Coke 5%
17. Do you feel exercise plays a significant role in the rehabilitation of heart patients?
    Yes 100%
18. Do you feel marathon running offers cardiovascular immunization?
    Yes 75%
    No 25%
19. Do you feel miles per foot are directly proportional to longevity?
    Yes 60%
    No 40%